George Müller

George Müller

A Life of Prayer and Compassion

Faith Coxe Bailey

MOODY PUBLISHERS
CHICAGO

Edited by Kevin Mungons
Interior design: Erik M. Peterson
Cover design: Faceout Studio, Tim Green
Cover portrait copyright © 2024 by NaxosUSA/Shutterstock (301113038). All rights reserved.

ISBN: 978-0-8024-3519-4

Originally delivered by fleets of horse-drawn wagons, the affordable paperbacks from D. L. Moody's publishing house resourced the church and served everyday people. Now, after more than 125 years of publishing and ministry, Moody Publishers' mission remains the same—even if our delivery systems have changed a bit. For more information on other books (and resources) created from a biblical perspective, go to www.moodypublishers.com or write to:

Moody Publishers
820 N. LaSalle Boulevard
Chicago, IL 60610

1 3 5 7 9 10 8 6 4 2

Printed in the United States of America

Contents

Preface

After George Müller died in 1898, the *New York Tribune* called him "an eccentric philanthropist with unbounded faith in prayer." The incredulous newspaper tribute described a man who "never asked the contribution of a penny," yet raised millions of dollars to care for the orphan children of Bristol, England. By *praying*.

During his lifetime, George Müller's ministry attracted the attention of many Christian leaders, including Dwight L. Moody, who met Müller while traveling to England in 1867. "The great orphan schools of George Müller are at Bristol," Moody reported. "He has 1,150 children in his house, but never asks a man for a cent to support them. He calls on God, and God sends money to him. It is wonderful to see what God can do with a man of prayer."

Faith Coxe Bailey wrote this brief biography for Moody Publishers in 1958, based on Müller's 1873 autobiography, *The Life of Trust: Being a Narrative of the Lord's Dealings with George Mueller.* Bailey's account has sold more than 275,000 copies to date and continues to challenge a new generation of readers. In preparing this newly typeset edition, we spelled his name as *Müller*, the German spelling of his name and the way he preferred it.

George Müller didn't like to talk about himself and didn't like the idea of a biography. He eventually relented, hoping that his life experiences would encourage others: "The greater the difficulty to be overcome, the more will it be seen, to the glory of God, how much can be done by prayer and faith."

1

Trouble at Home and School

When George Müller heard the carriage door slam, he knew his father was very angry. George stopped, halfway down the broad stairs, waiting for the oak door to fling open. For two days now, he had been waiting for his father's carriage to race up, spitting the gravel on the Heimersleben Road—waiting more fretfully than fearfully, feeling like a prisoner in his own home.

The door swung back, and his father stamped in. "So, you young jailbird," his father roared up at him. "You don't even have the decency to hide."

George stared straight down into his father's face. "You might have paid my fine a jot faster," he said.

Now his father was at the bottom of the steps, his hand gripping the newel post. "And miss the chance to teach you a lesson in honesty and respect! *Nein!* Well, what did a month behind bars teach my son?"

George's lips tightened; the corners of his mouth quirked downward. He shrugged. "That the meals in German jails are terrible."

The newel post shuddered in Herr Müller's hand. "But they're better in the village inns, *ja*? What did I raise—a common thief? Run up a bill and then sneak off without paying a penny!"

"Somebody didn't give you the facts, Father. One innkeeper took all my best clothes to pay for my room."

"So you try to escape out the window from the next one, eh? What were you thinking of?"

"Just a good time. That's all."

"Maybe the police taught you about a good time. Also some respect for authority."

"Police! Ha!"

"You're a no-good at sixteen. If your mother were here—" Herr Müller broke off. "*Ach*, she's been saved two years of misery. And where were you the night she died? Carousing around the street—drunk!"

Herr Müller's arm flailed out, and he grabbed for a cane, hanging on a wall rack. Then he thundered up the stairs, two at a time. "Maybe this'll teach you respect for authority."

George stood stolidly on the stairs, not flinching, but within him a terrible rebellion boiled. Did one man have the right to cane another man? Servant and owner? Father and son? Why was there always someone to say, "Do this"? Father, teacher, innkeeper, police. Would it always be this way? Did it have to be? Then his father jerked him sideways, and he bounced against the wall.

"Show me something to respect!" George shouted. "You're nothing but a second-rate tax collector, grateful for the crumbs off the province table! I should respect you?"

The cane pointed straight up at the beamed ceiling. "I'll teach you!"

Watching it, George thought, *Someday I'll be free. Free of my father, free of every man, free—* The cane cut through the air with a whistle and sudden sharp pain. Again, and again, and again.

Back at school in Nordhausen, the caning and the springtime skirmish with the police were only unpleasant memories. And not entirely unpleasant. They made good telling over a mug of beer.

The next two years and a half slid by, with Latin, Hebrew, Greek, the classics, and a good deal of beer at the Nordhausen village tavern. When George was nineteen, he was accepted at the University of Halle. Walking up from the Halle railway station, clattering along over the cobblestones, sniffing the violets and the old books that sold side by side along the main street, he realized he was now officially a student of divinity, properly accepted by the Lutheran Church of Germany. It was his father's wish.

Even so, he felt freer than he ever had. Setting his knapsack on the pavement, he stopped to admire the sturdy old stone wall that cut the city in two, a leftover from medieval fortifications, he guessed. Well, the old wall wouldn't box him in. Divinity student or not, he would do exactly as he pleased.

One night, late that fall, the barmaid served the fourth round of beer to the students at the long table. Right across the road from the university, Der Grüner Tisch did a bustling business with students. The air under the rafters was choked with biting tobacco smoke, and three young men pounded on the long green table in wavering rhythm. Suddenly the door opened.

Somebody shouted, "Here's George Müller. Now the fun starts. Only divinity student who pawns his watch to pay his card debts more often than he reads his Bible." Everybody laughed, and the table-pounders threatened to splinter the wood. George scraped a chair across the stone floor, squeezing into the crowd at the table.

"Herr Müller who says he's studying to be a Lutheran minister. Don't listen to him. He's really a jailbird!"

"All right, Emil. They all know me. Where's my beer?" George squinted happily through the smoke along the table. Here were his university friends, his drinking companions since the fall. But at the end sat a stranger—a stranger who looked familiar.

"Emil, do I know everybody here tonight?"

"*Ach*, stupid me! Here is Beta. Down here. He's new. Beta, this is George Müller, who just last week drank five quarts of beer at once and—"

Beta ducked his head to peer along the table. His voice had a hurried, eager sound. "I know George Müller."

George stared back at the fellow, hearing him say, "Don't you remember? We went to school together."

Swiftly, George flipped past classrooms in his mind. Halberstadt? Nordhausen? Why did the fellow sound so eager?

Then an unpleasant picture of a hymnbook and a Bible snapped into place. Now he remembered Beta! A goody-goody if there ever was one. Wouldn't cheat on an exam. Went to church every Sunday. Didn't object to naming off your sins right to your face. Didn't drink! Yet there he was at Der Grüner Tisch with a mug of beer in front of him. George's lips tightened, and he looked the other way.

"Beta, of course, I remember now. Ah, there's my beer. Say, did I interrupt a story when I came in? Let's have the rest of it."

Actually, it was George who told the next story.

". . . so I just slung things around in my room and made it look like a real robbery. Everybody felt so sorry. Every one of them stopped in to say I didn't have to pay back a penny of my card debts. Besides, they took up a collection for me. So I doubled my money."

When Der Grüner Tisch closed long after midnight, George helped head the three table-pounders toward their lodgings, shouted good night to Emil and the rest, and started down the road alone. But to his surprise, Beta trotted right beside him.

All evening, the sight of the fellow had made George uneasy. He was sure he knew why. Now Beta said, "George, I want to be friends."

"I know." For a minute they clattered along the cobblestones in silence. Then George added, "So—do I." It was something that he hadn't admitted to himself until that minute. Now he knew that he didn't want to take the words back.

Beta grinned. "I'm surprised to hear it. When you knew me before—well, I guess I was a pill." What was Beta saying? "But everything's different now."

"Different?"

"Before, back at school, I looked up to you."

"Looked up to me? You called me a sinner."

Beta's words spilled out. "I envied you because you were so good at cards. Because you weren't scared of teachers, or police, while I hung around on the fringes. Going off to prayer meeting with my Bible."

George felt baffled, fooled. "You mean now you're through with prayer meetings and all that?"

"No, not through. But I want to live a little too. When I found out that you were here at Halle, I thought if I could be friends with Müller, then maybe I could learn how to laugh and be happy and—"

Underneath the flickering streetlamp, George stopped short and threw back his head and laughed.

"And Müller thinks—if I can be friends with Beta—I can learn to be good! What a crazy fool!"

"You—want to learn to be good?"

Already George was wondering at his own feelings five minutes before. But he tried to explain. "Beta, I'm a divinity student now."

"Because your father says so."

"Wait. Be practical," George said. "The church is fussy. Drink too much, gamble too hard, and you're pushed off into some forsaken parish nobody wants."

Under the streetlamp, Beta was saying, "Oh!" soundlessly.

George went on. "That's not all. Half the time, I'm sick and tired of this silliness. But I don't know how to get away from it."

Still Beta stood there as if he didn't understand. In a way, George himself didn't. "So Beta, I thought you would teach me. But instead—"

"We can be friends anyway?" Again, that pathetic eagerness.

George nodded. "*Ja.* I guess. We will let the fates decide."

"Decide?"

"Which way we go. Your way—or mine. Who teaches whom? The fates decide. Or the *Devil!*"

Later, walking along toward his lodging alone, George looked up at the sky. The university buildings bulked gloomily against the blackness. He knew that if he wanted a decent parish, he had to change. Maybe Beta would help him find his way. Or maybe not. Briefly, he wondered about God, whom he hadn't really considered since Confirmation Day five years ago.

For some reason, his thoughts jumped from God to his father. He shivered, drew his coat tighter around him, and started up the stone steps to his lodging.

2

Welcomed as a Brother

The passports in the back pockets of every one of the five pairs of leather breeches striding out of Halle were unquestionably illegal. To get them, George Müller, his friend Beta, and the others had produced letters signed by their parents. But the signatures were all forgeries! George had forged his father's name with a flourish and malicious delight. And now all five were jubilantly on their way to Switzerland, their Alpenstock spikes clinking on the cobblestones. Why waste your summer stagnating in the boredom of your hometown? Holidays were meant for exploring the horizon's mountain peaks, for sampling foreign wines. So George had argued, and he had convinced his friends. Now with his broadbrim hat shoved jauntily on the back of his head, he was heading the party on its summer hike to Switzerland.

"Don't let George get out of sight," the fellow in the rear called ahead. "He's holding the purse. Can we trust him?"

As he shifted his knapsack from one shoulder to the other, George heard the coins jingling in the leather pouch. Beyond any doubt, the climb up Mount Rigi would be most rewarding!

In and out of villages, up and down mountain paths, through valleys—the five pairs of sturdy legs in their high woolen socks flashed by. When the boys were thirsty, they guzzled Swiss wine. When they were hot, they dove into mountain pools. When they were tired, they tumbled down in a field and slept until they felt like going on.

But often, long after the fellows were snoring in the hot sun, George was wide awake. And one day, propped up lazily against a tree trunk, he turned his head and looked cautiously over at Beta. But Beta—his blond hair rumpled, his face twitching from side to side to escape from the ants—was fast asleep. They all were, sprawled full length on the grass, knapsacks thrown down beside them.

Alert to the rhythm of Beta's snores, George leaned forward soundlessly, reaching for the leather pouch on the grass beside his knapsack. Opening it, he pulled out five smaller leather pouches. As Beta's snore hung in midair and faded out, George looked down sharply. But Beta's eyes were closed, and an ant tracked placidly across his forehead.

George moved hastily, but not a coin in the leather pouches jingled. He yanked the first small pouch open, and dipping in his fingers, pulled out some coins and transferred them all in one soundless motion to the second pouch. The knot of the third pouch's drawstring was stubborn. George bit at it nervously, then swiftly felt for the largest coins and slipped them also into the second pouch.

"Well, Müller, you're a sly one!"

His hand jerked away, then moved back again to play with the pouch string casually. He did not turn his head.

"Beta? Thought you were napping."

Beta yawned shudderingly. "Birds sing too loud. What were you doing?"

"Nothing." The pouches were back on the grass again, plump and tidy.

"Well now, you were!"

"So that's your business?" George flicked a blade of grass against his lips.

"Working when the rest of us were napping, I mean. Catching up with your bookkeeping instead of loafing. You're a good fellow, George."

Flick—flick went the blade of grass.

"Glad we let you hold the purse." Beta gulped back a yawn. "I hate anything to do with figuring and adding."

The corners of George's mouth turned up in sudden pleasure. "If you hate figuring and bookkeeping, don't worry your head about it. Some of us happen to have a little talent for money."

"Be glad of it, Müller. It might come in handy someday."

The blade of grass paused in midair. George eyed his friend acutely. But Beta's eyes were closed, his mouth was open, and he was getting ready to snore again. The little leather pouches dropped into the big pouch, and George knotted the drawstring. Sharp use of this talent for figures was getting him across Switzerland for half of what his friends were paying! Well, somebody had to hold the purse!

• • •

In the fall the forty-three-day holiday hike made good bragging at the long table under Der Grüner Tisch rafters. And always, Beta was there beside George, slipping him the cue for a funny story, laughing loudest at his jokes, reminding the barmaid when George's mug ran dry.

But sometimes, alone in his lodging, drinking his breakfast coffee, nibbling at his breakfast biscuit, George remembered wryly how the friendship had started. His curious flash of wanting to reform! It had been so foolish. Nine hundred divinity students at the University of Halle, and he wasn't any worse than any of them! Yet, it had all turned out well, after all. Beta had learned to drink like a man—well, almost—and cheated quite capably at cards. Beta was a good sport.

In November—the fall George was twenty—he and Beta sauntered from Der Grüner Tisch, and, shivering in the wind, hurried down the alley. At their usual corner, Beta peered up nervously as George said good night. "Meet you tomorrow. Like always? Right here?"

"No, George! There's something else," Beta blurted out. "I mean, I promised a friend of mine—man named Wagner—" Beta stammered. "I've known him for quite a while. Even—even before I met you. Now—lately, I mean—I go over there about once a week."

"Wagner has a card game?"

"No." Always when Beta was upset, his eyes bulged as if he were going to burst. Now they pushed out in agitation. "Look here, George, when I told you I wanted to live it up a little, I didn't mean I wanted to turn my back on everything forever."

"Go on."

"It's a prayer meeting at Wagner's!"

The strange term fell between them on the cobblestones almost with an audible echo. "A prayer meeting!"

"Don't make fun of me, George. We pray, sing hymns, hear a sermon."

He looked ridiculous, there in the shadows, his eyes popping. George put on a shocked expression.

"Sermons! And not in church? There's a law says you can't."

"It's a printed sermon. Somebody reads it."

"Then the law just covers you. This Wagner must be a daring soul. Maybe I'll meet him someday."

Beta only looked miserable.

Feeling cheated and deceived, George had an impulse to humiliate Beta, to make him pay for his turnabout face. "Tomorrow, in fact! We'll meet here. As usual. But we'll have prayer meeting instead of drinks." He turned away and then he whirled back. "Who knows! Maybe the wind blows my way after all. Maybe I'll learn something from your goodness after all, Beta!" And he laughed all the way to his lodging, remembering Beta's face full of misery.

Wagner's house was tucked into a long row of gray stone houses on a side alley in Halle. But its double gables gave it a friendly look, almost as if it were nodding with hospitality. The front door was friendly too, twice as wide as its neighbor's doors, its oak paneling curved at the top. A few men in substantial cloaks entered the wide door as George and Beta came up to the house. George felt more curious than teasy.

Beta introduced him to his host in a diffident, embarrassed sort of way. Wagner pumped his hand.

"I welcome you as a brother, Herr Müller. Whatever you are, whoever, as a brother. Now find yourself a seat and a hymnbook. We're about ready with the hymns."

In the library, the substantial-looking men had drawn their chairs into a circle. Perched on an inadequate little stool in the inner ring, George folded his arms on his chest belligerently and stared around the room. Not a man there looked pale and saintly, he noticed. They dared to be nonconformists, had the nerve to meet in houses and read sermons when the state church frowned on it. George studied them with the same attention he might have given to a new novel by Molière, or a new, untried kind of beer.

In front of the great desk, Wagner stood up to make an introduction.

"... welcome all our visitors tonight and pray God's blessing on our souls. Brother Kayser, will you ask God to be with us tonight?"

From where George was, it looked for a long minute as if Brother Kayser had fainted. He stood, and then turned his back to the circle, facing his chair. His knees shot forward slightly, then buckled. But no one jumped to steady him. In a moment, he was kneeling squarely on the wooden floorboards.

George stared in fascinated amazement. A nonconformist kneeling in public?

Then Brother Kayser prayed, and it seemed to George that he was talking to Someone who moved into the room and stood in great power so close to this man that he had to submit in a physical way.

"... for Christ's sake. Amen." Never before had George Müller seen any man kneel down to pray.

Afterward as he wrapped his coat around him, he had a question. "Why, Beta? Why was he kneeling?"

Beta's eyes darted first to Wagner, then back to George. "Don't tease, George. It's always done. At least here. That's why."

"Not where I've been. But why?" He fumbled with his coat. Then he answered his own question. "I know why. He had to kneel because he wanted to tell God that he was humble and human, and that God was almighty and all-wise. He was showing his awe, his fear, his adoration, Beta!"

"Something like that."

"What a man he must be to do that!"

Wagner blocked the doorway, helping people into their coats, grasping hands. "Remember, Herr Müller, house and heart are open to you. Come back."

"To prostrate yourself before the all-powerful God. This is true worship," he thought out loud.

Wagner's hand paused on the doorknob. "Herr Müller?"

"Herr Wagner, what I saw in your house tonight, I'll never forget. A man who knelt to pray to his God!"

There was almost nothing to say to Beta on the way home, and George left him with relief at the corner. At his lodging at last, he walked through his neat, bare study room without lighting a lamp. Crossing over to his bedroom, he sat down in the darkness.

What had happened to him? Because he was curious, he had walked into a man's house expecting to sing a few hymns absentmindedly, and pick up a few phrases for goading Beta later.

What was there about a man kneeling on the floor beside a chair to shake him this way? Suddenly, he knew. It was because that man showed with every muscle of his body that he worshiped, feared, and really knew the living God. What kind of a man! And what kind of a God!

This was it, of course. For years—since confirmation—he had known the facts of the atonement, had understood perfectly that Jesus Christ had died on the cross to save a guilty world. But this atonement had never lived, because to George God had not really lived. He understood that now.

And because he had seen a man kneeling to pray, he had seen God also.

At the window, he stared back at the gray university buildings beyond, fingered the unwashed breakfast coffee cups and crumbled the stale biscuit crumbs. Then he crossed back to his bed, and with stiff motions, he knelt.

The floor felt uncomfortable and cold to his knees. He did not know at first whether to bury his face in his arms or to stiffen his elbows on the yielding mattress.

But it didn't matter. He flung his arms straight out on the coverlet and throwing back his head, his eyes wide open but unseeing, he prayed, "When you kneel like this, low before the Highest One, meek before the Omnipotent One, then God is real." He sighed. "At last! God, tonight I am Yours!"

He stayed there on his knees for almost half an hour. Then, he got up, a little woodenly, and sat down again on his bed. He knew that something wonderful had happened to him. For a second he thought about his father, wondering if he would be glad or sorry when he learned about it. He assumed he would be glad, and then for no explainable reason at all, George Müller sighed.

3

Choosing to Be a Missionary

The slim girl in the depths of the overstuffed chair in Wagner's library twinkled flirtatiously at the gilt-edged mirror across the room. Her fingers caressed her silk skirt, and it sighed and whispered in the empty room. Picking up her bonnet, all white and pleated and starched, she tipped her head, tried on the bonnet, and tucked up a curl, still smiling into the mirror. She took off the bonnet and fluffed up her hair. Just then the library door opened.

"Well, George Müller," she said. "What kept you so long?" she pouted.

"Put your bonnet on," George answered. "It reminds me of angels' wings."

With her eyes on him, the girl—Ermegarde—drew on the bonnet. "I expected you lots sooner. You know very well Papa leaves early. I want to talk to you."

"I had to see Wagner," George told her.

"Didn't you see enough of old Wagner at prayer meeting to-night?" She sat down on the overstuffed chair, and the bright silk skirt fanned out about her. George remembered a rainbow in Switzerland, and a drawing he had seen once of a peacock. He said soberly, "I was returning some missionary papers."

"Missionary papers! Is that all! Oh, George, you're so solemn!" She patted the arm of the chair, smiling up at him.

He perched on the chair arm. "They're the most exciting things I've ever read. Ermegarde, listen to me. What is happening to our world in this century and the last is what happened in the Book of Acts. I never knew a thing about it before. All of a sudden, it seems to me that Christianity is like a flower holding its seeds to itself, and suddenly a wind comes along and—puff! There's a seed here, and there's one, and there's one over there!"

"Gracious, George, you don't need to wave your arms around like that! Watch out for my bonnet!"

George scarcely heard her. "The mighty wind blows and that man, John Williams, off to the South Seas. And what's his name— John Wesley—sails off to the United States. And William Carey to India."

"I know about John Wesley. He's a strange one. They say he didn't want to get married and settle down ever."

Repelled by the girl's attempt to narrow down a mission call to a matter of a man's opinion of marriage, George bounded up and put the room between them. "Ermegarde, listen. Since last

November, my whole life is changed. And reading those missionary papers—can you keep a secret?"

She pouted. "Your secret, yes."

"I've told God that He can send me to any mission field in the world." He watched her face, but it was as expressionless as an empty saucer. "Ermegarde, I'm going to be a missionary."

Now that the words were said, he wanted her approval. What kind of a girl was she anyway? The prettiest female at the Saturday night prayer meeting, that much he already knew. He had noticed her first because of the way she let her eyes rove during the singing of the hymns until they met his, asking little questions. Wagner had said that her father came to prayer meeting only for the coffee. But his daughter?

"That's nice." She had evaluated his life's commitment in a flat voice. Then she stood up. "I hear Papa out in the hall. He'll be wanting me to go." She fussed with her bonnet ties. "Gracious, George, I hope when I see you next Saturday, you won't be so solemn!"

Crossing the room, she stood very close to him for a moment, and she smelled very clean and sweet. He thought about flowers in a Swiss meadow—and then she was gone. The library door closed behind her. George was left alone with the uneasy knowledge that the joy about his new decision was no longer very intense.

In the weeks that followed, he never doubted that he had obeyed the voice of God. Where he would serve, when he would go, who would send him—these were questions he would answer later. Now it was enough to know he had changed his vocation. He would not be a minister of the proper state church. He would be a missionary.

Yet each Saturday at the Wagner's prayer meeting, his joy diminished. His conviction wavered. Always Ermegarde was there to tease him. "Gracious, George, don't be so solemn! Come over to the harpsichord. I know a rollicking new song." She sat very close and linked her arm in his when they were together in the library. And while he was with her, he felt as if the other—this feeling that God had spoken to him—were just a dream.

Later, he walked back to his lodging in gloom.

Passing the massive bulk of the Halle orphanages, he heard a child crying. He hurried on, but the child's lonely cry followed him down the alley. Alone in his lodging, he tried to pray.

On his knees, he buried his face in his arms. But no words came. Neither did any thoughts. He could not reach out and touch God. God wasn't there. Then he realized He hadn't been there for days.

What was wrong? The sound of Ermegarde's teasing laugh filtered through the room. "Gracious, George, you're so solemn!" His fist hammered the mattress. He couldn't go to sleep without praying.

Getting up from his knees he found a dusty prayer book on his shelf. Opening it at random, he read: "Grant me, I beseech Thee, almighty and merciful God, fervently to desire, wisely to search out and perfectly to fulfill all that is pleasing unto Thee.

Order Thou—" But he was hardly listening to himself. He hurled the book against the wall.

"God, where are You?" he cried out. "Did I find You to lose You again? What have I done?" But although he listened now, he heard no answer at all, just the echo of the teasing laugh and the memory of the child crying in the orphanage.

It was another Saturday night, and George was again in Wagner's library. Ermegarde wore a dress with a collar like a fluffy April cloud. The voices at the front door were very far away. Suddenly overwhelmed by the poignant cleanness and sweetness, he bent down and kissed her. He said, muffled, "I love you, Ermegarde."

She looked quite pale. "I—oh, George, I think I love you too!" He kissed her again. Then she said, "If only—"

"If only what?"

"All this talk about being a missionary."

"All this *talk*!"

"Then you are serious."

"Serious!"

"I—George—I don't think I'd fit in at all."

Holding her close, listening for her papa coming down the hall, he murmured, "You just think that now. You'll learn. We'll learn together." He felt more confident of that then he ever had.

But her answer knifed him. "I don't want to learn. Missionaries are so—shabby and poor."

"Is it your father, Ermegarde?" he asked, holding her away, studying her face.

"Not all Papa. George, I do want to have nice clothes and good furniture and a carriage I'm not ashamed to drive through town. I wouldn't be happy if I didn't. I just couldn't marry a missionary."

"But I'm going to be a missionary. And I—I want you to marry me." He hadn't intended at all to say it so positively. But it had been said.

She fussed with the strings of her bonnet. "George, do be sensible. Why don't you think about teaching? Or law? They're both good professions."

"Are you asking me to give up my calling?"

"I'm not asking," Ermegarde retorted. "I'm telling you. Really, George, Papa wouldn't let me throw myself away on a missionary. And I wouldn't want to. You think it over. You'll just have to choose."

"Choose?"

"Yes. Give up something." She smiled up at him and took a step closer. But he did not kiss her again. He felt as if he had been slapped, and turning, he held open the library door.

Stumbling along unhappily to his lodging that night, he passed the orphanage again. From out of the cavernous many-storied building, a child screamed. George rued his choice of a path and hurried on.

The next two weeks were very black. On Saturdays, he saw Ermegarde. They talked, they argued, they kissed. If he could only make her feel the fierceness of that November day when he had first prayed. But sometimes it was a dream from which he had awakened long ago. As for the mission field—. But he couldn't give up Ermegarde.

Winter dragged bleakly by, and in the spring he met Hermann Ball. Hermann wore cheap clothes with a gentleman's air, and handled himself at a banquet with finesse. George appraised him quickly as a young man from a good family, yet Hermann was introduced as a missionary. Later after coffee, he explained. He was serving in Poland as missionary to the Jews there.

His eyes glittered when he described the ghettos. George could smell the sick babies, the moldy wash houses. He asked a dozen questions about Poland, about the Jews, about Hermann himself.

Then reluctantly, Hermann told his story. Yes, his family had money. His father was a wealthy merchant in East Germany. No, they didn't understand how a man can throw away a career for Christ. He had been disinherited.

What a great thing he had done, George started to say. Hermann stopped him.

"You don't balance two things. You don't say—here is a life with the Polish Jews, poor, maybe even disagreeable. And here is my family with its carriages and its carpets and its rich Christmas puddings."

George was listening closely.

"You say—God wants me to do this. So that's the only way I can be happy. No, Müller, it isn't that I've given up so much. I've gained more."

"It's still a big sacrifice. You gave up so much."

"Don't make me out a hero. In my place, you'd do the same thing. Well, wouldn't you?"

In his own ears, George's voice sounded hollow, "Yes, yes, I suppose I would!"

In Wagner's library after the Saturday prayer meeting, Ermegarde was wearing a new dress that rustled like tender spring leaves. But George tried not to listen. Remembering Hermann Ball, he knew what he had to say.

"Listen to me, Ermegarde. Make your choice. Choose to marry a Lutheran missionary or choose to be what you already are, a shallow little beauty."

She stopped, watched her gilt-framed reflection, and turned wide-eyed to George. "This is a new George."

"In God's strength, I am."

She teased. "And a new kind of God."

But he did not smile. He stepped back. "Ermegarde, what will it be?"

"I won't marry a missionary." She stamped her foot, and the "tender spring leaves" sighed.

But George was angry at the woman, angry at her for being so beautiful and so empty. "Then you don't marry Müller."

The library door opened, and George flung himself out, past the girl's father, down the hall, past Wagner pumping hands at the doorway, and out into the night.

It seemed to him that the night air had never been so clean, and he gulped it gratefully. "You don't balance two things. You say—God wants me to do this." Again, God was so close he could almost touch Him. "Thank You," he breathed, and went on his way down the cobblestone alley, praying. It seemed as if he had turned a sharp corner, and the mission field was in sight just ahead.

• • •

The carriage rocked mercilessly along the valley road from Halle to Schönebeck. Sweating in the June heat, George squirmed against the cushions. In the tight breathlessness, he was hearing his father's voice; he was parrying with his father, debating, convincing.

It was desperately important that George convince his father. He was traveling home on a vital errand; in his pocket was an application to a German missionary training institute. Unless his father's name appeared on the application, it would not be valid. As the stage jolted along, George wove phrases and arguments into a compelling dramatic scene.

That there would be a scene, George was sure. When he had written home about finding God, his father answered with sarcasm. What an unpredictable man! Angry when George let the Devil lead him around by the nose, and angrier when he turned his life over to Christ.

Unpredictable except in one thing! George knew he could predict that his father would oppose him! Something of the old rebelliousness, the old feeling of wanting to break loose that amounted to panic, surged up. His independence! Well, if he had ever been dependent on his father, it was now. Everything hung on his father's signature.

So the stage jolted on, and George leaned back and dreamed a disjointed, feverish dream.

At home, the supper was a good stew, but all through it Herr Müller evaded discussion.

"Well, George, you hardly touched the stew at all. What bothers?" And then, "Your mother—she should be alive. She makes you eat. Too thin, you are, my son."

But George had only one thing on his mind. "Father, I came to Schönebeck for one reason. I want to ask you—"

His father interrupted, frowning. "Hush. Your judgment, it is no better. In the kitchen, the servants, they have the ears to the door. Now, no more words. Tell me, my boy, how does the reading in Cicero please you this year?"

After supper in the parlor, George laid the application blank on the mahogany table and demanded his answer. The explosion came immediately. "When I say *nein*, I mean *nein*!"

"All right, you mean no. But tell me why."

"*Nein* is enough. I will not put my name on your paper."

"Because you know it will keep me from transferring to the missionary institute?"

"*Ja.*"

"Why? Why don't you want me to be a missionary?"

"*Nein* is enough."

"But you always wanted me to be a *minister*."

Now his father was on his feet, tramping from window to mantel, making the dusty door draperies shiver with the breeze. "Aha! A Lutheran minister, *ja*! A man whom the good people in the village look up to and respect. *Ja*, and fill up the larder at Christmas holidays. A Lutheran minister earns a nice wage! A nice house he gets, warm and clean with lots of rooms."

"You think of that?"

His father tramped past him; hands clenched behind his back. "*Ja*, I thought of that. Only a fool wouldn't. Four years' university, you take. Now you are twenty-one, and to this missionary place you go and lose everything."

"But it's a specialized—"

"For what specialized? Specialized for turning out fanatical missionaries who know nothing but to starve with the heathen. Who don't have a penny in their pockets to send to their poor parents."

Then George saw the trap. He understood in a flash the reason for the firm no. He could have forgiven a lack of understanding of his call. But this was deliberate selfishness.

"You're asking me to—" he began.

His father cut in. "Who has a better right? Who put shoes on your feet? Who gave you pocket money for your card games? Who bailed you out of jail in Wolfenbüttel?"

"But not for payment—"

"You are so sure! Selfish! Self-centered! Ungrateful! A missionary, bah!"

Then his father stalked from the living room, the door draperies dancing behind him. Upstairs, the floorboards creaked from wall to window, from window to wall, as his father paced, and little flecks of plaster floated down from the ceiling. An hour passed, and still he paced. Downstairs, George sat and wondered what he could do now.

But in the morning his father was different, gentler. He had aged overnight, or he wanted George to think so. His fingers nervously traced the carvings on the mahogany chair, as he said, "My son, understand a father. In one afternoon, an old man's dreams you tore down."

"You're not old," George said with stiff lips.

"His hopes, his little securities. I was to be so proud to say, *There goes my son.* Now what must I say? *My son, he is a missionary, but he does not know the Bible says, 'Honor thy father and thy mother.'*"

"It also says, 'Leave all and follow me,'" George answered. Then earnestly, George asked the question he knew was inevitable, "Father, what do you want me to do?"

The answer came at once. "When you are through at the university, a nice church you find. Settle down. Marry. Have a nice parsonage. Children. For the old father, a room. A nice warm room with wide windows."

"For a nice warm room with wide windows, you'd have me say no to God?"

"I wouldn't have you chase to the end of the four winds to convert the heathen and not a penny for your sick, aged parent."

George bit his lips. His father wasn't sick, and he wasn't old. He had money in the bank. He was well-to-do.

"An old man needs his security." His father brushed at his eyes, vaguely.

"Father, may God forgive you for what you do to me today. May He forgive you for making me choose."

"And what do you choose?"

"I've promised God, and I'll keep my promise. Somewhere there's a mission field that needs me. I will go there. I will not be a Lutheran minister."

"But the application blank—I tell you, I won't sign it."

"Then don't sign it. I'll finish at the university and make the best of it. But wait. You'll never have another chance to say I take everything and give nothing." His father stared back at him, not speaking. "I won't take education from you if I can't pay you back the way you ask."

"You talk big. What can you do?"

In the still room George's voice sounded too bombastic, too melodramatic. But he had to make sure his father understood. "I won't take money from you again. Never! As long as I live!"

On the way back to Halle, George was sharply aware of what he had done. He realized that at last he was independent of his father. In all the world, he was dependent on no one. He felt free, like a prisoner just out of jail.

As the carriage bumped into Halle, he could hardly wait to tell Beta. The exuberance of this independence was a wonderful thing. From now on, he was dependent on only one Person in the whole wide universe. That was God. And that was how he wanted it to be. As he alighted from the coach in Halle, he wasn't sure in his own mind which was the greatest, his independence or his dependency on the almighty God.

It wasn't until the coach door slammed behind him that he realized that he had hardly any money at all, certainly not enough to pay his term's bills.

4

Study and More Study

At first, the thought must have seemed preposterous to young George Müller. Preposterous and nervy and more than slightly insane. Ask God for his bread and butter and money to pay his school bills? What right did a 21-year-old fellow, still in school, have to ask God anything at all, and especially a request as homely as that!

Yet the thought came. And during his first week back at school, as he inquired about a chance to earn some money, it persisted. Since he had given up Ermegarde in the spring, God was again very real whenever he knelt to pray. Real and close enough to talk to about almost anything. So the absurd thought churned in his mind.

One morning, eating breakfast in his room, he shoved aside his coffee and biscuit and knelt, elbows on his study chair propping up his thin, bony face.

"God," he said out loud, "You know exactly what I've done and what this means. You know what I need. Money to pay my rent, buy food, get books, and settle up for the coming term. I'm depending on You, God, to see that I get it. In Your own time. In Your own way. I'll wait." He hesitated for a minute, listening. "If it is Your will. In Jesus' name. Amen."

A little later, there was a knock at his door. He opened it to find Dr. Tholuck standing there. With him was a stranger. "Doktor Charles Hodge, an American professor from Princeton University." Tholuck bowed.

"Come in, come in!" George swept books and papers from the only comfortable chair.

"Now, George, we get right to business," Tholuck said, waving the American to the chair. "Dr. Hodge needs to learn the German. I tell him I know a bright young student who speaks both the English and the German. In fact, I tell him that you will tutor."

George studied the American, standing with his hands in his pockets, smiling amiably. "My English isn't like Coleridge or Wordsworth." He spoke somewhat laboriously in the unfamiliar language.

"Neither is mine." Hodge laughed. "But I don't want to write poetry. We'll make out."

"I'll be glad to oblige Dr. Tholuck. But time is a problem."

"You name it. I'll be there."

"Well, my class schedule is pretty full. And besides that—"

George felt embarrassed, but he knew he had to explain. "This term, I have to work besides. That's why I have less time than—"

The American frowned and turned to Tholuck. "Is my English that bad?"

Dr. Tholuck shrugged, and looked a little helpless. "George, my boy. This is not clear? Tutoring is work."

"I know that, but I mean—"

"Strictly business," Hodge boomed. "Standard rates, whatever they are, and then some. In fact, double them. We're in a hurry. Want eight hours a week."

"Eight hours a week! For the whole term? You'll pay?" George blurted out. "Why, that'll cover about a fourth of a whole term's expenses!"

"Great! The others will pay the rest."

"The others?"

Hodge shrugged, then laughed. "Tholuck, I must be speaking very badly today," he said.

"George, what Dr. Hodge means is this. Three of his American friends want the tutoring too."

"We study together, pay you separately. Fair enough?"

"Fair!"

Tholuck patted George on the shoulder. "You see, my son, what we hear is true. Americans always have the money."

But George shook his head. "Tholuck, this time you're wrong."

"How's that?"

"It is God. It is God who has the money."

When the door had closed behind Tholuck and the American, George sat down again at his study table and let the impact of what had happened break over him. Unbelievable, irrational as it seemed, God had answered his prayer for money!

What was it Beta had said to him only the summer before in the meadows in Switzerland? "A talent for money, George!" Cards, cheating, lying, and stealing! What a great talent had been his! How much better it was this way. He bowed his head: "How much better! Thank You, God!"

So George Müller got through the school year. He took no money from his father. His tutoring lessons paid for almost everything.

And for a part of the year his lodging was covered by a free room for divinity students in the local orphanage. Once George had looked at the monstrous, six-storied orphanage with its narrow, cramped windows and had shuddered. Once passing the playground in midday had depressed him.

But now that he knew the story of how the home was built, he was strangely fascinated. A. H. Franke, university professor of theology a hundred years before, had no money, no wealthy family, nothing but faith that God answered practical praying. So he had prayed, the money had been given, and he had built the immense orphanage for two thousand children. The tale fitted in strangely with George's mood that year, and he accepted the free room without reluctance.

Later in the year, George asked something else from God,

something as important as bread and butter. "God, where do You want me to be Your missionary?" was his question all summer, and into the fall.

For a chilly November night, there was nothing like a dish of Tholuck's hot beef stew. After a day at the library, George was dipping into a plateful gustily when Tholuck spoke, and his spoon stopped in midair.

"*Ja.* I say London needs you, George. Pass the salt."

"Needs me? What would London do with me? I'm a German, Tholuck. Through and through."

But Tholuck pressed on. "What do you know about London, George?"

"About what anybody can read. The popular novels, mostly. Grimy little orphans slaving in the factories. Littered streets. A lot of mud and poverty. And it's foggy. That's all."

"But this isn't all. There is so much more to London."

"Then maybe I'll see it someday," George said with a grin, and ladled more stew onto his plate. "Now Tholuck, stop joking with me. You know, I'm still disappointed because the Russian war with the Turks canceled my appointment to the Bucharest field. Of course, I'm waiting for any sign of God's leading. But I know that missionaries don't go from Germany to London."

Tholuck was very grave. "Can you be sure, my boy? Many kinds of Londoners there are. You hear about the London Society, *nein*? The London Society for Promoting Christianity Amongst the Jews? There are Jews in London just as in Poland,

and in America, and in Germany too. And they all need Christ."

Take Christ to the Jews? How had Tholuck known so much about his thoughts? Now he had a dozen questions. Did Tholuck know he had seen Hermann Ball lately? Did he know how he had agonized with Hermann over the news that his health might force him to quit his mission to the Polish Jews? Tholuck nodded. He knew all that, and he also knew that George had immediately started studying Hebrew on his own.

But didn't Tholuck wonder why he had done nothing about this interest? Again Tholuck nodded. Because George had been signed up for Bucharest.

There was one more question. How could he know whether the London Society would consider him? Tholuck had an answer. "Because I know an agent. Myself! Say so, and I submit your name at once."

George's spoon clattered into the stew. "You, an agent? Tholuck, is this the way the Lord speaks?"

"You tell me, George."

"But so suddenly?"

"Ah, my son, it isn't sudden. Not at all. Hermann Ball, missionary to the Jews, teaches you how to give up the girl you love. You go to work to study the Hebrew just because you love it. Always you love the English, and know it well enough to teach."

"Yes, but—"

"At the last minute, a war keeps you out of Bucharest. Why, George, my boy, this is not sudden business at all."

After Tholuck's letter was sent to the London Society in December 1827, George realized the impatience that boiled within him. He wanted an answer the next week. But a month dragged by. A new year came; the first month of 1828 passed by. Still he heard nothing. Still nothing in February.

Finally, on a March day, Tholuck caught up with him as he crossed the university campus. "I heard from London."

"What did they say?"

"Very little," Tholuck said, remotely.

"Very little!" George exploded. "I've been waiting three months."

"They are considering your name. They sent me a packet of papers. Questions you are to answer about yourself." He interrupted George's protest. "*Ja*, I wrote them about you. But they must have details."

A wild frustration shook George. It wasn't fair for these British executives to keep a man waiting, just because he was hardly in his twenties and a German besides. "What kind of men are they?" he shouted. "Don't they take the word of a man who says God has called him? Isn't that enough?" Wildly, he snatched at the papers Tholuck held out and darted off.

But that night, with a pen that sputtered along the page, he filled in the details, and posted the answer to London. Again, he waited. For three more months, he heard nothing at all. And when the letter arrived in the middle of June, he roared across to Beta's lodging.

He had been accepted by the society as a missionary to the Jews in London, but only on one condition. He must first serve six months' probation.

"Study six more months. Why do I need to study? I'm a university graduate. For two years I've been plugging along on Hebrew."

Beta tried to calm him. "Specialized techniques."

George cut in. "I'll tell you what it is. These society directors, they're dictators! Men that lay down rules without thought of humanity! Men that bully with their authority! Men like my father!"

When he said it, he was filled with the old rebelliousness. The Wolfenbüttel innkeeper who had him jailed. The police who had locked him in a cell. His father who had always demanded so much. What right did the London Society have to demand six months' probation? He was ready to step out in Piccadilly Square at once to proclaim the only way of salvation.

Independent, was he? He wouldn't be if he said yes to the London Society. "I'll be under the thumb of another dictator."

"But what can you do?" Beta irritated the wound.

"I can say no. Does God want me to waste six months of His good time? No, Beta! No, no, no!"

He hurried back to his own lodging and sat by his study table, growling for a while, and then reached for his pen to write the letter to the London Society.

"Thank you for your letter," he wrote, furiously. "I will be in London as soon as I get my passport. Yes, I accept your terms: six months' probation."

5

A Six-Month Probation

"All the way across the channel I've been telling myself that when Herr Direktor hears how the hand of God was in my coming at this time, he'll forget the foolishness about rules and let me start my work at once!"

In the London Society's front office George crossed, then recrossed, his legs for emphasis.

"Yes, yes," the director of the London Society said vaguely, and smiled at the wall at a point above George's left ear.

None of the London street grime had seeped into the front office. It was as gray and clean and aseptic as the lank Britisher behind the desk. Across the room, a clerk, humped on a high stool, wrote in his ledger.

"When Herr Direktor hears about the miracle that brought me here, he'll say, 'George Müller, you don't have to wait six months before you preach to the Jews. God wants you to begin right now!'"

Tensely, he told his story. Six months before, after he had mailed his acceptance, he had applied at once for his passport. But he had been turned down, told flatly that he could not leave the country until he served his term in the German army. Sure that it would be simple to get exemption as a missionary, he wrote to the province president. His exemption was refused.

Panicky, he appealed to the king of Germany himself. From the king he got another no. Friends in the Berlin courts tried to push through an appeal, but they were no help.

Then the miracle happened. First, he developed a cough and fever. When he was over that, a small blood vessel in his stomach burst. Midwinter, he had reported to the army doctor for his physical examination. But the doctor told him sadly that he wasn't strong enough to be a soldier, that he didn't think he would ever be, and promptly issued a certificate that discharged him from military service—for life!

"A miracle got me out of Germany," he finished. "That is why I can say God wants me to start work at once!"

The director refocused his eyes in the general direction of George's face. "My dear chap, you are a university graduate? I ask because so many of our fellows are not. You have studied Greek, and I presume you comprehend French?"

George nodded. "All the Classics. Before I was twenty, I was reading Cicero in the original. For recreation."

The director's eyes slid off to the spot on the wall again. "Yes,

yes. Mr. Müller, you seem to have an extraordinary background for a young fellow."

George's heart pounded. Then the icy Englishman had understood after all. This casual approach was just his way.

"You know Hebrew?"

George beamed. "Love the language."

"How many university hours in Hebrew?"

"Not any really. I loved it so much I studied it on my own," George added hastily. "Bought some books and—"

"Yes, yes," the director broke in, coolly. "Now George, you are acquainted with the Aramaic?"

"What?" George asked.

"No Aramaic?" Across the room, the clerk's scratchy pen punctuated the words. "Tell me, do you have difficulty with the rabbinic characters?"

"I haven't—that is—" Suddenly, George was angry. "I don't need the rabbinic alphabet to tell the Jews in Piccadilly Square that Christ loves them. I can give them tracts, tell them what happened to me."

But the director interrupted. "Now then, give me your attention. Here is our program. For the first six months, we'll concentrate on Hebrew. And if you peg away rather faithfully about twelve hours a day, in six months you'll be ready. Most of our new chaps are."

George leaned forward. His throat felt tight. "Now is the accepted time; now is—"

"You will master the German-Jewish Old Testament in the original rabbinic alphabet," the director intoned. "You will want to commit many portions of the Hebrew Old Testament to memory. And you'll want to start right away. Tomorrow."

The clerk's pen grated on, and the office walls squeezed in on George. Only the Wolfenbüttel cell had been narrower. Once again, he had lost his independence. He had come to England to be trapped, caught by a rigid man behind a desk, hemmed in.

From a distance, he heard the director's voice, "I say, why are you staring at me, George?"

"Because just now you look exactly like my father."

• • •

But he buckled down to his probation and its schedule of twelve hours' study a day. He hated almost every minute of it. Shut away in his lodging with his books, he felt he had sinned against God. From his window he could see gabled roofs, and the heads and shoulders of workmen and women off to market. "Forgive me, God," he prayed, "for mumbling the alphabet when they're going to hell out there in Houndsditch and Hyde Park. God, keep my mind clear! Twelve hours a day is too much. And keep my soul clear, God! My studies must not crowd You out."

To him, the rabbinic characters looked like the tracts of an ink-drenched spider. He got thoroughly entangled in Aramaic grammar. At night he recited characters of Isaiah in Hebrew until they burned into his brain; in the morning, he had forgotten.

When he was tired, the Hebrew grammar made less sense than a nursery rhyme.

Grammar and alphabet. Aramaic and Hebrew. Learn in the original Isaiah 53 and Daniel 3! Eight hours. Ten hours. Keep at it, George!

But the maze in his mind grew more cluttered. His head ached, and his back ached, and his neck; George was very sick.

He let the doctor bleed him. After the bleeding he felt hazier, weaker, and no better at all. He choked down rhubarb by the quarts because the London doctor declared that the bitter plant was a cure. But when he was better, the doctor gravely announced he needed more than rhubarb. Even another bleeding wouldn't help.

"Get away from the soot. For the lungs, for the whole body—" The doctor made dramatic, wide gestures. "Get the best medicine any doctor today knows—sea air!"

"But I can't leave London," George protested. "I'm behind with my studies now. Delayed and—"

"You'll be delayed more if you don't," the doctor said, tersely. "Son, get yourself to the coast and put some salt air into those lungs."

So in September, George packed himself off to England's west coast. He came to the little seaside village of Teignmouth in Devonshire County, and he stayed, gulping in the salty air and complaining about the new delay in starting his great mission. He made his complaints to his new friends, the Christians in the fishing town's Ebenezer Chapel. One of his friends was a minister in nearby Shaldon—Henry Craik.

From the start, the friendship was an odd one. They were about the same age, twenty-five, both university graduates, both committed to giving the world the gospel. But George found something distasteful about Henry, with his sparse wiry hair that stood straight up in fierce wisps, and his wrinkled thrown-together clothes. And Henry was as cautious and conventional in his living as he was sloppily eccentric in his clothes. George thought his caution just a plain lack of trust.

But George soon knew what Henry thought of him. "Look here, old chap. Don't be so on your nerve. Go back to London and settle down and cooperate with the society. They've been functioning a good many years, and they jolly well know what they're about. You toe the line they draw for you, and don't go off on some tangent of your own."

Well again, George traveled inland to London. But the fog and soot stifled him. The society's regulation was choking his spirit. Fidgety and nervous, he wrote a tormented letter, asking that further study be canceled. Couldn't he be put to work at once?

He waited five weeks for an answer. The society remained silent. *Men had no right to stamp out the flames of Christian passion*, he fumed in his room, watching the crowds push by in the streets. He bundled together his tracts, pushed his Hebrew Testament into his pocket, and rushed from his lodging out into the street.

For the next few weeks, in a kind of wild fury, he stopped Jews in the square and in the markets, pushing at them invitations to his lodging for conversation about God. At the fringe of the Jewish community, he preached Christ on a street corner. When he found fifty young Jewish boys who liked to hear him read the Scriptures, he organized a Sunday school class.

By Christmastime he was tired. He was tired of the city's filth, and he wanted to walk along the Devon coast and feel God's power hurl the waves up on the shore.

But in Devon, he didn't find the peace he was looking for. Walking along on the sand, he watched the waves break again and again on the same rocks and the same sand, and it seemed as if they were wasting their energies. As the white spray lashed up against the rocks, then dropped down, spent, he wondered how much like this exhausting, frantic winter sea had he been. His thrashing about with Sunday school classes and tracts, all on the sly. That monotonous repetition with the studies that never seemed to move anywhere.

But the sea told him something else. It stretched out before him, flat and green and free to be itself until it met the heavens somewhere in what seemed like infinity from the Devon shore. The rough air was suddenly heady. A gull drew black circles against the clouds and then was lost. To be as free as the sea! To be under no one at all but God! By the sea at Devon, George Müller made his decision.

Later, he and Henry Craik walked along the shore road, and George tried to explain. "Henry, I've made up my mind. It isn't the will of God for me to give all my energy to His chosen people."

Henry drew his fuzzy eyebrows down. "What?"

"To the Jews, first, yes. But also to the others! That's what God wants me to do. Henry, there are thousands in England—Gentiles, church members—and they don't know this wonderful Redeemer of ours. I'm going to preach to them too."

Henry stopped short, bracing himself in the wind. George said, "Well? You stare at me as if I'm an irresponsible idiot."

Then Henry exploded. "Have you forgotten one little thing? You're responsible to the London Society—the London Society for Promoting Christianity Amongst the Jews."

"I haven't forgotten. I'm writing to the society today to tell them that God is calling me to take the gospel to all people everywhere. That I will minister wherever, however, to whomever God tells me."

"You're telling them that?"

"More besides. I'm telling them I'm willing to continue as their missionary, but from now on I'm taking my guidance not from any man—"

"George, don't do it."

"But from God Almighty alone," George finished.

"They won't understand. You might as well say you won't cooperate with them." Henry's eyebrows went up and down.

"Just so. A servant of Christ has just one Master. Don't argue with me, Henry. I've made up my mind." George started to walk along the road again, his eyes on the far line of sky and sea.

Beside him, Henry sputtered. "Don't do it, old man. They'll cut off your support. You're a stranger in the country. A stranger without funds."

With his eyes still on the horizon, George answered, "I don't think they will. These are godly men. They'll know how I feel about letting God guide me." Then he added, "Besides, as long as I put the kingdom of God and His righteousness first, then I'll have funds. These things will be added unto me. I've proved it once. I'll dare to prove it again if I have to."

Beyond the horizon lay Germany and his father. George shivered a little in the January wind and jingled the coins in his pockets.

He had just 5 shillings left. Enough to mail the letter to the London Society, and not much more. He turned and, with Henry, walked back to the fishing village.

The letter was posted. Later, he learned that the London Society had called a special meeting almost at once. The last week in January 1830, he opened the letter that announced their drastic action. It read something like this:

> Resolved, that Mr. Müller be informed that the committee cordially rejoices in any real progress in knowledge and grace which he may have made under the teaching of the Holy Spirit.

But they consider it inexpedient for any society to supply those who are unwilling to submit themselves to their guidance in missionary operations.

Therefore, the committee cannot consider George Müller as a missionary student for the Society any longer. But if more mature reflection causes him to change his opinion, they will readily reconsider the matter.

6

The Pew Tax

A nd so, I accept your call. I'll stay in Teignmouth. Pastor your chapel. Preach the truth to you as I see it. But only on one condition!"

From behind the pulpit of the Teignmouth chapel, George Müller watched the women's faces within their bonnets grow wary. His call had hardly been unanimous. There were mutterings that the young foreigner would ruin the church with his frank talk about unpleasant things like believers' baptism. Already, some families had left.

But when the deacons asked him to stay on as their minister, George heard God's voice. One day, a foreigner in a strange country, rejected by his mission society. And the next day the minister of a church in a small Devon seaport, prosperous with salmon fisheries and good British currency.

But as he gripped the pulpit, pulling the right English words from his mind, he wondered if it had been God's voice. Should he give his life to a church of eighteen members? Let eighteen people tie up all his energies and his thoughts?

"Only one condition," he repeated. The fishermen and their wives, the innkeeper, the deckhands waited. "I won't guarantee how long I'll stay. I retain the right to leave when I want to."

The bonnets ducked and turned while the fishwives clucked sideways at their husbands, then bobbed up again like so many whitecaps on an angry sea. "I'll preach here as long as God wants me here. But when He says move on, I'll move. The very next day if He says so. That's the condition."

He intoned the benediction, then moved down the aisle to shake hands in the tangy wind at the door. As the people filed by, he heard their whispers, as melancholy and as penetrating as a sick gull before a storm.

"What do you make of that mouthful?"

"The cheek of the foreigner!"

"Here today, gone tomorrow. What if my man went about his fishing like that?"

"Pity he isn't married. A wife'd say her piece about living one day to the next."

Let the fishwives mumble and smirk about what a wife would do to him. They didn't know the high price he had paid for his independence. No wife would ever speak her mind against his doing God's will!

• • •

The piece of paper had lain in his pocket so long that the scribbled name was a blur. As the carriage squeaked along the inland road to Exeter, he pulled it out, smoothed it down and puzzled over it. Hales? Sakes? Laher? He'd better forget Miss Paget's friend and hire a room at the inn, where he could be sure of a place to think quietly before he preached. It was enough favor to the woman to preach here in Exeter. Hakes! That was it. He leaned forward, raising his voice to the driver.

"Ever hear of the Hakes family?"

The driver nodded. "We go right by their place, sir. Want I should drop you by the gate?"

The Hakes' home was big, pretentious, and drafty. As George stood in the front hall, fidgeting with his leather case, he wished he hadn't come. Before the servant had disappeared, she had muttered something that made Mrs. Hakes sound like a bedridden invalid. He heard someone on the stairs, and, looking up, he saw a woman smiling down at him as if she had known him for a long time. Yet behind the smile, she was appraising him as she came briskly down the stairs.

She was about thirty-two or -three, he guessed. She was at least seven or eight years older than he and yet, in spite of this, he felt as if he could share a great many things with this woman.

"Mr. Müller?" The woman spoke as if she had a number of jobs to accomplish in a short time. "Let me take your coat.

We've been expecting you. Miss Paget wrote."

"Mrs. Hakes?" he asked, hesitantly.

The woman laughed. "Gracious, no! I'm not the mistress of anything as fine as this. I'm Mary Groves, companion, nurse, general handywoman. Here, I'll take the bag too. I expect you want tea. And a chance to rest. Come along in the parlor. We expect great things from your preaching."

What a refreshing female, George thought, following her into the parlor. There was no blushing when she said she wanted to hear him preach. Over tea, she talked about the problems of beginning a new church with the logic of a man. She summarized Mrs. Hakes' sickness and told him about her own family, but she didn't embroider the details.

Yet George only half-listened. He was wondering why he should find a woman with such a long, broad nose so fascinating. "And my brother is a missionary," she finished.

"Your brother? Not Anthony Groves?" She nodded. "The one that went off to Persia without a penny of pledged support? Just went off—?"

"God wanted him in Persia. He believed that," she said, matter-of-factly.

So this was Groves' sister. No wonder she had such a frank, fearless way. "I admire your brother a lot," George said. And then he wondered why it sounded so lame, so inappropriate, to say to this woman. Suddenly embarrassed, he repeated awkwardly, "I admire your brother a lot, Miss Groves."

The sermon that night was not his best. Walking to church alone, he had thought of Ermegarde, who had been pushed to the back of his mind for so long. He was back in Germany again, at the university, at Tholuck's prayer meeting, in the little library, on the sofa listening to Ermegarde giggle. When he got up to preach, the German was still in his mind, and his English came in jerks.

But after service, Mary Groves, there with Mr. Hakes, stood in front of him, not taking his hand. "You preach what the Bible says, George Müller, like you did tonight. He'll always talk through it."

Back at Teignmouth, he tried to tell Henry Craik about the Exeter excursion. "Her mind was as crisp and bright as—as that sand in the sun," he said. Henry Craik's bushy eyebrows darted up, then lowered gloomily. George wished he hadn't said anything at all.

"I say old chap, are you going back to Exeter?" Henry asked.

"I—I said I would. They don't have anybody to take their midweek meeting."

Henry smiled.

"She's past thirty, Henry," George protested. But he wanted to add, "The most honest woman I've ever known. And past thirty isn't old."

That spring, he discovered that a man can fall in love with an honest look and a frank mind just as soundly as he can with a merry giggle. He forgot the troublesome eight years between Mary and him. Ermegarde no longer floated teasingly out of the past. Yet all spring, he fought against his love for Mary Groves.

Would marriage make him a prisoner? Would it root him to one spot, smother him with babies and kitchen smells and fireplace wood and a scrubby backyard vegetable garden? Would marriage chain him so he'd never be free to answer God, whenever, wherever He called?

"Of course, it won't," Mary Groves declared with conviction. "Christian marriage doesn't trap anybody. It will give you wings."

He and Mary were married in October 1830, at Exeter. That afternoon they shared communion at the Hakes' home, and in the evening they traveled by carriage to his lodging in Teignmouth.

Right away, there was trouble. That first week, George kept his thoughts bottled up within him, but when Henry Craik stopped by for tea, the cork popped out.

"Well, Henry, what do you think?" He and Henry were waiting for their tea at the kitchen table, while Mary nursed along the hot water at the wood range.

Henry spoke gloomily, "I'm not taking sides in a family quarrel. Especially when it hasn't been a family a week yet."

But George went on. "Be honest, Henry. How does it look to you?" He gestured toward the china cupboard in the corner, and the parlor beyond.

"Better than I thought it could. Mary, you've worked miracles in these old rooms." She came toward them with the tea. "Curtains here. A picture there. A miracle, Mary."

Mary set the tea down. "And don't forget the sweeping and the scrubbing, Henry. All week I've been at it. The dirt—"

George slammed his hand on the table. Make fun of him, would they? "Stop it, both of you. That's not what I mean. Henry, give me an honest answer. How does it look to you? What do you think of all this fancy silverware?"

Henry gulped down his hot tea. A blob from the edge of his cup fell on his vest. George sputtered on. "This ostentatious, ornamental—?"

More tea on the vest. "Well, it doesn't look like you, George." Henry's eyes had the audacity to twinkle.

"Does it look like our Lord?" George snapped. "Our Lord who owned nothing?"

Mary's voice was level, unemotional. "Henry, the silver belonged to my family. When I moved, I brought it along."

Henry's small eyes darted into the living room beyond. "And the tapestry hanging in the parlor?"

"Yes."

"And the china in the cupboard?"

"Yes."

George interrupted. "'Lay not up for yourselves treasures upon earth, where moth and rust doth corrupt.' Who said that?"

Henry looked hard at George. "George, old man, I like nice things. I jolly well don't think it's a sin to like them. But my wife didn't have very much silver in her dowry. Yours did. What are you going to do? Give your wife back?"

George looked away in fury. How could Henry laugh at his convictions?

But Henry went right on. "What do you want Mary to do, George? Take these things back to her folks?"

George couldn't keep from boiling over any longer. "More than that. I want her to get rid of them completely, forever. The Bible commands it."

"The Bible? Where?" Mary asked.

"Luke 12:33. 'Sell that ye have, and give alms.'"

Henry shook his head violently. "Look old man, that doesn't mean—"

"It doesn't? It says!"

"You want me to sell my silver?" Mary spoke very low.

"George, you don't have any money but your salary. This silver is like money in the bank," continued Henry.

"Exactly. And the fine china too."

"My china!" exclaimed Mary.

George slammed his hand on the table, and the cups danced. "I fell in love with the girl whose brother dared to go to Persia without a shilling. But I marry a fine lady who puts possessions first. Sell it all and give the money to the poor. That's what God told me, and we must obey Him."

For a moment, Mary studied him. For a moment his heart stood still, and he prayed, aching a little inside. Would this woman he loved—but hardly knew at all yet—fetter him so that he couldn't keep pace with God? Then as he prayed, he saw her mouth grow tight and serious. Very quickly, she spoke. "All right, George," she said. "You decide."

Nights, the ocean was a constant roaring, sometimes muffled with fog, sometimes strident with wind. In the first few weeks they lived together, Mary and George left the supper dishes cluttered on the table and rushed out of the house to walk along the beach road and inquire about the ocean's mood. There was no place better for talking.

"You don't hate me, Mary?"

"No."

"You aren't afraid of what I'll do next?"

"George, I trust God too."

"I don't deserve you, Mary. Sometimes I wonder if I should have married at all."

"George!" In the moonlight, she looked almost beautiful. He wondered that he had ever thought her nose too big.

"I mean—"

He groped for words to tell her. "There is something inside that tells me something wonderful is just ahead. Something fearful too."

She was shivering a little, and he put his arm over her shoulder as they walked along. "Once before I had this feeling. When I told my father I wouldn't take his money. It's a feeling like a bird."

"A bird!"

"A feeling you're flying-up-up. A feeling that you're altogether free."

She pulled away from him. "All right," she said, "tell me what God has said to you now." She had made it so easy for him. It was the pew rents, the miserable system of renting the best seats in the chapel to the people who could afford the best price. The system put people like deaf Mr. Kennerly, who was poor, behind a spot where he couldn't read the lips of the preacher. The system was hardly Christian. George felt it had no place in the church. He saw only one solution. The Teignmouth folks must abolish pew rents at once!

"They'll never do it, George. It's been a custom for years."

"They'll have to."

"But George—" Mary spoke slowly as if she were trying to explain something he didn't understand. "The pew rent is how the church is supported. How your salary—" She stopped. George knew she understood.

"You see?" he asked. "You see why they have to do it?"

"I don't understand, George."

"If the pew rents are my salary, then it's up to me to decide whether or not to—"

"—to rent the pews." She stopped on the road, and George could feel her rearranging her emotions. When she spoke, she only said, "I understand, George."

It was a week later, and they were hurrying along the road toward the chapel.

"You have the nails, Mary?"

"Right here in my pocket. What about the hammer?"

"I have it. And the key to the chapel."

Underneath the November moon, the sea looked brittle and

cold. George wondered if Mary were sorry about anything. Then they were at the chapel door.

"George, do we have to go in yet? Look at the stars. So bright. And there's a gull. Watch it twinkle in the moon. Don't go right in. It'll never be quite the same."

Now she was talking like any other woman. He turned the key, creaking the heavy door open. "It'll be better," he said. As she walked soberly past him, he caught her shoulder and swung her around until she faced him.

"You do believe that? That life will be better than ever after we do this?"

She nodded. Swiftly, his lips brushed her forehead. Then he lit the lamp. "Hand me the box. And the nails."

It took less than five minutes to nail the small wooden box at shoulder height on the back wall of the church. It took less than that to hang the sign over it.

"How lonely it is here," Mary said, above the pounding.

"No! God is here!" George hammered away.

After the sign was secure, he stepped away from it and squinting a little in the flickering light, read it aloud, wanting to shout, feeling a greater triumph, a wilder exultation than he had ever known.

Henceforth, the minister will be supported only by contributions placed in this box by generous Christians.

He will not at any time nor for any reason ask any man for financial sustenance. He will ask only God.

Behind them, the heavy door closed. "How do you feel now, George?" Mary whispered.

George wet his lips. He could taste the salt in the air. "Mary, I feel as if I had been trapped by something I loved and knew I shouldn't love. As if now I'm suddenly set free of everything and everybody to be the person I should be. The person God wants me to be. That's how I feel. As if something wonderful is going to happen to me. But what it is, I don't know yet."

7

Moving to Bristol

Julia Thornsberry pointed along the road that crooked its way down to the Teignmouth docks, said something about January weather being good net-mending weather, and shut her door tight against the wind. Hunching his shoulders against the blast, George hurried downhill to the docks. Into his back, the wind stuck a chill finger to prod him along, but he needed no nudging.

Now that he had made up his mind, he was in a desperate hurry.

Propped up against a post, his legs dangling over the dock's edge, Deacon Thornsberry alternately took a stitch and blew on his hands to warm them. As the dock clattered under George, the deacon looked up and grinned. "Well, pastor, you turnin' fisherman too?"

Glad that the deacon's red cap had been so easy to spot against the gray boats, and a little breathless from the wind, George approached him. "Not me. I came to find you. Your wife said you'd be down here on the wharves."

"January's good weather for net mending, pastor," Thornsberry grunted. "Now see this here 'un. She's good for another season's wear if I stitch up the rips and—"

But George had no time to waste on talk about fishing nets.

"Deacon—" he interrupted.

The deacon went right on, "Tighten up her seams a mite." Then he stopped and blew hard on his hands. "You want to see me about something special, pastor?"

George nodded. "It's the contributors' box in the church."

The deacon shoved his net to one side and shifted his weight. He looked up at George. "Pastor Müller, any time you want to change your mind back, you speak the word. We'll take down the box with no talk at all, and put you back on a regular salary. You hear me, son?"

George sighed. This was going to be harder than he feared.

"Now, you sit down beside me. Let your legs dangle and hold the net for me. Like so. That's the fellow. Tell you the truth, pastor, that wife of yours has been lookin' peaked lately. You folks gettin' enough to eat?"

Even to himself, George's voice sounded too loud, too protesting. "Deacon Thornsberry, until Mary and I started out together on our great adventure with God, we didn't know what happiness was!"

The little grooves along the deacon's cheeks deepened.

"Ummmm, well, I say no woman's gonna flourish gettin' down to five shillings in the house like you two did two months ago just three weeks after you started your—uh—great adventure."

George wished he had never spied the deacon's red cap. With the talk going this way, it was going to be six times as hard to state his business.

"You want to see me about something?" the deacon urged. "Watch the net. It's sagging."

"Deacon, God has proved Himself. People are generous." As he talked, he crumpled and uncrumpled a great corner of the fishing net in his fist. "But—" Then, in a rush, "Deacon, you know I promised God never to ask any man, anybody, for money as long as I live. Nothing will break that promise. But—"

Even before the deacon answered, his hand reached for the pocket of his great jacket. "Not another word. Happens I have a mite extra on me today and—"

Now he had done it. He had ruined his high resolve with clumsiness. "No, wait. I don't want to ask for money. I came down to ask you—just to ask you to have a good system for collecting the money from the church box. Like once a week." He hurried on, stumbling over the English words in his desperation to make the man see that it wasn't regret for his bargain that had forced him down here. "If Mary and I could count on the money—no matter how much or how little—on one certain day every week, we could plan. That's all." God, help this man to see it wasn't lack of trust that brought him here, just plain ordinary common sense and practicality.

"Now was that all you wanted, pastor?"

George nodded.

"Well, if that's all, don't look so down in the mouth about it. Don't think twice, pastor. Of course, we'll do like you want. Empty the box once a week and give you the money. How's that? I can't foresee any reason why we couldn't oblige that way. No reason at all."

• • •

The key turned and the Teignmouth chapel door swung back. Deacon Thornsberry picked his way in, groping for the lamp, and muttering, "Dark as a haddock's belly in this church. Where's the light?"

The gas flames hissed up and the fisherman walked directly to the back wall. With his knotty knuckles, he rapped sharply on the bottom of the contributors' box. From the depths, a few coins jingled dispiritedly. "Huh! Don't sound like much more'n a few buttons."

Unlocking the box, he lifted up the lid, and scooped in his hand. "Now what do you make of that? Hardly enough for a man to clench his fist around. Mighty embarrassing, I'd say."

Later, the deacon thrust his leathery old face into his wife's and argued in a voice that matched the booming ocean. "I tell you, Julia, I'm not going over to the pastor's with this pitiful handful of coins. It's an embarrassment."

But Julia did not retreat. "You promised that boy every week."

"You don't seem to figure what an embarrassment this is to the Ebenezer membership, Julia."

"It was the same last week and the week before. And after what you promised him. Why, you haven't been over to the Müllers' with a shilling for almost three weeks."

"Julia, it tells a sorry tale for our people."

"Shame on your miserable pride. That poor laddie and his little wife may be starving, for all you know. He asked for the money once a week and you're letting him down."

"Better he should think we let him down instead of knowing the truth."

"What's the truth?"

"What's it look like to you? It looks to me—and God forgive me for saying so—but it looks to me like the heavenly Provider has let George Müller down for reasons of His own."

• • •

The key turned and the Teignmouth chapel door swung back. George Müller picked his way in, groping for the lamp, muttering, "Black as the Devil's heart in this church. Where's the light?"

The gas flame hissed up, and he went directly to the back wall and the contributors' box. He had never done this before, but even though he had sneaked out of the house without telling Mary where he was going, he did not consider this breaking his bargain with God. He would not take a single coin from the box.

He would wait, as he had agreed, until the deacons brought the money to him. They could take their time, and he'd never ask for it. But he had to be assured that God at least had not dawdled with the answer.

He rapped on the bottom of the box, and only the sound of knuckles against thin wood came back to him. He rapped again, harder, but he heard no coins dance.

"Nothing!" He said it incredulously and rapped again. "Empty! Nothing!" He turned out the lamp, and again the church was completely black. He stood still, looking across the empty pews to the altar. "So it has come to this," he said out loud. "Nothing for George Müller from God."

At home, in the cramped little back room that they used for a bedroom, George stood a long time looking down at Mary asleep. In those few moments, he punished himself without mercy. What had his faith done to the person he loved best? Would his dogged trust in God starve her? Was his determination to depend on God, not man, no better than irresponsibility? Punished, but not remorseful, he knew exactly what he must do next.

He shook Mary awake. "Get out of bed."

She woke up reluctantly. "George, are you sick?"

"Get your wrap." Sleepily, she groped for it at the foot of the bed. "We have to pray."

Now she was awake. "George, something's wrong?"

"Nothing's wrong," he told her solemnly. She slid from the side of the bed to her knees, and he knelt beside her. "Not if we believe

His promises. Pray with me, Mary." He took her hand. Then quietly, he spoke to God. "Father, all we are comes from You. All we have. This is the promise we hold to, and we won't give it up. If You are holding back from us because of some sin, cleanse our hearts. Speak to us. And then, O great God, supply our needs."

And about that time, Deacon Thornsberry lumbered out of bed and lowered himself into the rocking chair at his window. He called over to his wife. "Now don't be frightened, Julia. I plan to sit here at the window for a spell. I can't sleep no matter how I turn. Seems like I got George Müller on my mind, and I can't get him off. I was wrong to hold back that money on account of pride. Soon as sunup I'll get along over there with the coins."

The Müllers were eating breakfast when they heard the knock at the door. Even before he opened it, George had spotted Deacon Thornsberry's red cap.

"So I came right over," the deacon explained, wiping his feet on the threshold. "'Tisn't but a mite. One pound, eight shillings. I'm ashamed to hand it to you."

"This is God's money, deacon. Never be ashamed of it." George tried to keep his voice even, but his heart was singing. He didn't dare look at Mary, busy with the tea.

"It's funny," the deacon told him. "Seems like I heard that about not being ashamed before."

"Yes?"

"Seems like that was what went through my mind last night. Or maybe I heard somebody say it somewhere."

The corners of George's mouth quirked up in merriment. "Yes, deacon. I wouldn't be a bit surprised if you did."

And that was the way it went for George. When he got down to his very last shilling in April, somebody dropped a couple of sovereigns into Mary's handbag as she rode home on the train.

In November, he didn't have bread enough for his next meal, nor any money to buy it. That afternoon, a woman whom he had never seen before knocked at his door and handed him a loaf of her own fresh-baked bread.

By the end of the year, December 1831, George had received— from the church box and other donations—131 pounds, which was almost three times as much as the full salary he had accepted from the Ebenezer Chapel!

• • •

There in the kitchen, the cradle was beginning to look like something a baby might rock in without being either seasick or terrified. At first George had nailed on one rocker crookedly, and the cradle had twitched instead of rocking. But he was remedying that while Mary sat in the chair by the stove, stitching a small bonnet.

"George, don't spend all evening fussing over that cradle. You do have five more months to finish it. Don't neglect your sermon."

"No sermon tonight." He went on hammering.

"No sermon? It's Saturday."

"I'm not preaching tomorrow. Just talking."

Mary jabbed her thumb with the needle. "I wish you wouldn't.

You're not very good that way. What are you 'just talking' about?"

"No text." He wondered if he sounded casual enough. It seemed to him as if she could hear the crackling of Henry Craik's letter in his pocket. "No text. Unless maybe Matthew 28:19–20. 'Go ye therefore, and teach all nations.'"

"George, what are you thinking of?"

He put down the hammer, rocking back on his knees, crushing against the letter. "Mary, tomorrow I'm telling the folks at Ebenezer that my time with them is about up." Mary said nothing, but she suddenly looked pale. When she tightened her lips and whitened, her nose seemed very long, George thought.

"You know the agreement. When I want to, I can go."

"But not now." She flung down the bonnet. "I know what it is. It's plain human envy. Ever since Henry Craik went off to preach in Bristol, you haven't been the same!"

He weighed the hammer in his hand. She went right on. "You want to get down there in the hustle and bustle of that big city. George Müller, you are so human!"

"Mary, when did I ever say this sleepy little fishing village was the place for me? When did I promise to stay here forever?"

"But now! We're doing so nicely. God is providing."

"He can provide in Bristol too."

"So it *is* Bristol."

"I don't know." He couldn't tell her now about the letter.

"But it isn't just you and me anymore. It's the baby too. Or it will be in September."

"So the Lord can provide for one more Müller." He got up then and, with his foot, kicked the cradle out of the way. Suddenly, it seemed like a lumpy mistake, a bad piece of carpentry and a waste of his good time. The room seemed close, as if the walls were going to squeeze him. For a moment he couldn't breathe, and then his head began to pound. He felt as if he were trapped on all sides, and he knew that even if he went for a long walk, he might not feel any freer.

But outside, under the stars, he prayed. "Neither parents, nor authorities, nor wife, nor children, God! I rebel, God! Rebel from everything and anything that shackles me from walking along Your road."

Far from the house under a lamp, he took the letter that had been so bulky in his back pocket all evening and read it again slowly. Postmarked Bristol, England, written by Henry Craik, it said:

". . . Gideon Chapel here on Newfoundland Street in the heart of what will be slums in a few years. Here we could both preach and minister. And there is talk of beginning a new chapel, in a fine city neighborhood. We would share this too. It's work with great potential, George. They've called me, but rail against your ideas as I do, I've found I need your mystical dependence on God. We would work together here so well, George. How about it, old fellow? Why don't you come down and look Bristol over?"

George folded the letter into a small square. Well, Mary would learn to like Bristol, he was certain.

8

A Blighted City

The tumbled-down house, one gable askew, looked out onto a gutter filled with garbage; in the doorway a woman was crying. "Thankee, Pastor Müller and Pastor Craik, for the prayer and everything. Hit means *so* much to 'im, like we knew you always, instead of you just being 'ere in Bristol two months." She sniffled and dabbed at her eyes with a vast filthy apron. "The prayer means *so* much, even if 'e just lays there not talkin.'"

There was sympathy in George's words, but he backed down the crumbling steps as he talked. "Your husband's a very sick man. I wish we could stay longer, but—"

"I know 'ow 'tis. Just keep prayin', gentlemen. That'll do wonders." Before she had closed the door, George was on the pavement. Henry followed, slowly, running the tip of his finger up and down columns in a black notebook.

"We're frightfully near Kent's," he began. "Hadn't we better—"

"Henry, did you see that man's eyes?"

"We could pop up Hereford Lane, don't you know, and be there in a—"

George interrupted. "His skin. Henry, did you see his skin? Yellow!"

"Poor chap. He's in a bad way," Henry said absently. "I think we made his misery a trifle easier. I—George, whatever's wrong?"

Now at last, he had Henry's full attention. "Two years ago in London, it was the same. I saw it there."

"What was the same?" Henry fretted.

"That fellow in there—God help us all!" George wanted to cry out. "That man has cholera!"

"Cholera!" Henry croaked.

"It's come up from London. That's what. Spread from the epidemic there. And there's nothing in the world that can stop it."

Henry was rooted to the pavement; his wiry hair seemed to bristle in terror. "But if he—how many more, George?"

There had been dead bodies in the London gutters, and mourners who went in and out of the cathedrals so constantly they might have all been attending the same funeral. There had been a smell of pus and death in almost every house. "It spreads like fire," George said.

Henry's eyebrows worked up and down. "Cholera! An epidemic! It can't happen in Bristol, George."

And then he heard it. A single bell. It might have come from far out at sea, a simple warning to a fishing boat. But George had left the beach at Devon behind, and this far-off ringing had nothing to do with the placid life he had lived in Teignmouth. While he listened, hoping that he had heard nothing, the single bell was joined by another, closer, louder, with a throaty dissonance.

The funeral bells of Bristol!

"It's too late, Henry. Our epidemic has started. We've come to a blighted city."

And Bristol was a blighted city, that summer of 1832. The August sun rotted the garbage in the gutters. Even the pigs nosing through the remains were too miserably hot to root out their favorite morsels. Children found water of sorts running through the gutters and jumped in, up to their knees, to sail toy boats. Up and down the humped, pitching streets the cholera germs raced, like so many maggots discovering a pile of fruit. The flat-roofed Gideon Chapel on Newfoundland Street was as hot as a baking box, and the people who met to pray God's deliverance from the scourge sweltered inside like raisins in the dough.

It was a blighted city. It was no place at all for two young preachers who had just come to a new ministry, pledging themselves to serve the people of Bristol without a stated salary, depending on God and the good people's generosity for their coffee and cake and lodging.

But George Müller and Henry Craik *had* come to serve. The

epidemic did not stop them. They prayed with dying men. They sat in fetid rooms with feverish children, reading the Bible endlessly. And August blistered into September.

In September, George found himself confronted by a weary, hysterical wife. Standing squarely in the door of their lodging, she faced him. "George Müller, I won't move. You won't leave this house today."

He understood. These were terrible, frightening days for Mary. But God's call had to come before a woman's fear.

"Get away from the door, Mary."

"No."

He took her arm. "They're my people. I came here to minister to them."

"You didn't come to kill yourself. What can you do anyway?"

"Pray!"

"Pray! Every morning for two hours, you've prayed. Two hundred of you at the church. It hasn't stopped the epidemic."

"Don't say it, Mary. Nobody from the church has died."

Her voice rose higher. "Two hundred of you, praying and spreading germs."

She had no right. "I've heard enough." He pulled her away from the door.

"Don't think about yourself. Think about me. And the baby! The baby, George, in less than a month! Suppose you brought cholera home to me. What about the baby?"

He felt as if she had slapped him. "Don't—"

"Suppose you died. You talk about ministering to people. Do something for your own child, George. Stay home. Hide!" She sobbed wildly.

"I'm going out, Mary!"

"George, please. You'll die. You'll—"

He opened the door, and the funeral bells moaned over the city. "I'll minister to Bristol, as God called me to do. He never said, 'In fair weather and good health.' He said, 'Go to Bristol and work.' I'm sorry for you, Mary. But *this* comes first." The bells jangled in his ears as he pulled the door shut behind him and hurried down the street.

Later, he and Henry wearily dragged down Paul Street toward home. All day they had been with the sick and the dead. The flickering streetlamps turned the shadows of the house railings into dancing skeletons. "How long can we keep this up, old man?" Henry asked. "If only the Blaney woman hadn't died. The first of our little band. We prayed so hard."

Suddenly George stopped, steadying himself against the railing. "Henry, I feel dizzy. Stop a minute." There had to be an end to this. "I can't go on much longer. Only God can save us now."

"Only God," Henry echoed.

There in the deserted street, leaning against the railing, George began to pray. "Into Thy hands, O Lord! Here is Thy poor worthless child. If this night we're taken by the cholera, then our hope and trust is the blood of Jesus Christ, shed for our many sins. O God, help us!"

Henry's words were an echo. "O Lord, except You keep us to-night, we'll be no more in the land of the living tomorrow. Amen."

• • •

Bristol was plague-ridden until October. And then, it was all over. George and Henry were exhausted, but they were well. From the Gideon Chapel, only one member had died. On October 5, 1832, the two young ministers called a special service of thanksgiving for God's keeping.

As he prayed that morning, George had a very personal word for God. With the epidemic in its last writhings, his daughter Lydia had been born. She was straight, healthy, and Mary said she looked exactly like George.

Parish duties became normal. The new chapel, Bethesda, opened in a neighborhood slightly less foul than most of Bristol. For the next four months, life for George and Henry was a routine of preaching and calling.

But in January they received the letter that was written to reshape their lives. It was an invitation to sail at once to Baghdad as missionaries. Two hundred pounds, to cover traveling expenses, fell from the envelope.

Since he had been 20, he had dreamed about sailing off to a place like Baghdad, where the people wrapped themselves in exotic silks, and the men were swarthy, and the women mysterious, and the marketplace like nothing he could even imagine.

Exotic Baghdad, city of traders in ivory and perfume, city of oriental music. What a far cry from the Bristol slums!

As he made his parish calls, plodding through the slimy winter streets, he tried to think logically. He tried to pray. One late afternoon, crossing the city from home on Paul Street to the chapel on Newfoundland, he was deep in thought. Baghdad seemed so lively, so real. He even imagined he heard the Turkish traders shouting their wares in the marketplace.

"Hey, ya bloke! Give us a handout, what?"

But the trader had a Gloucestershire accent. George wheeled and found himself looking at a 12-year-old boy. "Hey, 'ow about a shilling, gov'nor?"

From behind an immense iron fence, the youngster grinned out at him. He stuck his hand between the bars. "Can't come out and get it, gov'nor. Ya see I can't. 'Ow about it?"

Behind the boy lurked a clay-colored monstrosity of a building, narrow windows like eyes squeezed shut to keep out any happy sights. This was the almshouse. The scrawny youngster shouting at him was some luckless orphan, fenced in until the law said he was old enough to go out and learn to be somebody's drudge.

Fishing in his pocket for a shilling, George remembered the huge orphanage in Halle, Franke's orphanage. But that had been different. This almshouse was as unkempt as a beggar and twice as forlorn.

Suddenly, wild laughter climbed waveringly to a high pitch and hung there. For a minute, there was nothing else in the city night but the boy's face, the fence, and the terrible laughter. Then it choked off. And began again, wilder, higher.

The boy shrugged. "Just an old looney, gov'nor. Don't be scared. Where's my coin?"

What good would a shilling do? George dropped it into the hand. The boy would grow up there, caged with lunatics and criminals, while George Müller slipped him a single shilling and sailed off to exotic marketplaces.

Sail off to Baghdad? No! He couldn't leave Bristol to dirt and disease and the Devil himself. Whether he could ever do more than a shilling's worth for Bristol's poor, he didn't know. But he was sure of one thing: he must stay and try.

After that, he was never again content to be merely the copastor of the two small chapels. In the instant he gave up Baghdad, he knew that God had something more radical and dramatic for him than the chapel ministry. At first, when he heard about the free day schools for slum children, he was certain that this was God's mind for him. So, from the money contributed to his support, he managed to squeeze out regular, sizable contributions to the organization that ran the slum schools.

But the schools never quite satisfied him, nor even pleased him. He suspected the doctrine of the sponsoring organizations. They preached that the world was getting better and better. They took contributions from anybody, Christian or not. When he tried to discuss it with them, they mouthed words like "tradition" and "expediency."

"God, I can't be happy working with human dictators, and I pray that is Your way of telling me not to be dependent on any man." Abruptly, he decided he could give nothing more to the schools.

But he did not lose his mission to the Bristol slums. Slowly, a new dream began to take shape.

When he tried to tell Mary about it, they were in the kitchen, finishing up the mutton. Her fork clattered to her plate. "George Müller, why'd you have to bring this up tonight? No, I don't want anything more to eat." Lydia, playing on the floor with a doll, inched over to the table, whining a little.

"Mary," George pleaded, "God is telling me to strike out on my own. To start my own day school. Share my vision."

"Vision!" she retorted. "More visionary than vision. Scriptural Knowledge Institute. I don't even like the sound of the name. Pompous."

"Forget the name. It'll do the job. Provide day schools for boys who can't afford tuition. Give them the right kind of Bible teaching too. And it won't be run by men who aren't Christians. This will be our own school, Mary."

She pushed her chair back. "I don't want to hear any more. Time for bed, Lydia."

"Mary, this is my calling."

She whipped around. "Your calling comes at mighty inconvenient times. Before Lydia was born, the epidemic. Now you talk about starting a school the week before the new baby." She began to cry. "Besides, you don't have the money."

George reached for her hand. "God will give it to me."

She pulled her hand away. "How do you know? Tell me the truth. How much do we have in this house right now? For rent and food and your school?"

"Right now?"

"Right now."

"One shilling. But Mary—"

"One shilling. That won't buy much more than a loaf of bread. One shilling to start a school. To give out Bibles. To buy tracts. To feed two children. George Müller, what are you thinking of?"

• • •

George and Mary's son was born on March 19. For a month, life in the Müller home on Paul Street turned on feeding time and bath time. But George had not forgotten his dream. God wanted him to stay in Bristol, and He had something more than the Gideon and Bethesda Chapels.

Late in April, he talked frankly about it to God: "God, I come to You in great presumptuousness. I believe You want me to start my schools. I believe the Scriptural Knowledge Institute is right. But if I don't get money soon, I'll have to give up my plans. God, if I could have twenty pounds—it's a lot, I know—I'd buy some Bibles and give them away. It would be a start."

Before the day was over, a woman came to the door. She handed George an envelope.

"I'm sorry it isn't more, Mr. Müller. But I—"

Five, ten, fifteen, it was twenty pounds. "Madam, do you want me to spend this for something special?"

"Beg pardon?"

"I don't use money given for one purpose for any other need. For instance, if you wanted my wife to have this for the house—"

"Well—" The woman hesitated. "Is it all right to say?" she asked timidly.

"Go right ahead."

"What I had in mind was—Bibles."

When the woman left, George wandered into the parlor, turning the twenty pounds over and over in his hand. Mary came in from the kitchen. "I heard, George. I'm sorry. I've been wrong."

"It's not a matter of wrong," he protested.

"It is. You've been right. The Scriptural Knowledge Institute— and those day schools—they must be God's will. Or He wouldn't have sent that money. It's a sign."

He could have kissed her. "I pray it is," he said.

"So do I. Let's pray together, George. Right now. Right here."

9

Praying for an Orphanage

He was a skinny little boy, and his ears stood away from his head like two sails in a wind.

But he jammed one hand into a torn pocket, rubbed his nose with the other, and defied the headmaster. "Won't do you no good to cane me, mister. I'm not taking books home tonight, anyhow."

The gaunt headmaster plucked at his underlip. "I don't understand your attitude, young man. Sneaking out without your books. Refusing to do your assignments."

The two ears seemed to quiver, and the small boy backed away as if he'd been slapped, "Please, sir, I wasn't sneaking. The reason it wouldn't do me no good to take books home tonight is because—"

The headmaster towered over the boy. "Well?"

"Because I'm not going home. Nor coming back to Mr. Müller's school, neither."

"So this is the gratitude you show your benefactors?"

"I can't come back, sir. Last night they took my ma away."

"Away?"

The bony hand rubbed the nose furiously. "Away to Newgate, sir. So I can't go home. 'Tis the almshouse for me, sir."

"You can't give up school," the headmaster protested. "You're too bright, Colin, there must be something—"

The small head shook from side to side, waving the two pink-tipped sails. "I know the almshouse, sir. Once you're behind that fence, well, you are, that's all. Won't be no school for me."

"Maybe later. When your mother—" the headmaster tried.

"No, sir, I don't think so. Please, will you say goodbye to Mr. Müller for me and tell him thanks? His school is bully, and I wish I could stay."

• • •

The straight walk from the day school to his home on Paul Street was quite short, and George was sorry he had suggested taking the roundabout way that dipped down to the harbor. The lanky legs of the headmaster were too long to make him a comfortable walking companion for a shorter man like George. But worse than that, he had nothing to tell on this long walk but a discouraging story.

And the walk along the docks could be exhilarating. The barrels of sugar and rice fresh from the West Indies, the ships creaking at anchor, the tropical tobacco mingling with the salt air, it was all part of God's magnificently wide world. Fifteen minutes at the docks always changed his perspective, made him immensely grateful for living in a wonderful world. At the docks, he forgot the filth of the city behind him. Here he could pray better for the people of Bristol.

But today, as George picked his way through the barrels and the boxes, he hardly heard the excited talk of the West Indians. The headmaster's story had spoiled the day.

"What good are schools if we don't have students?" George said glumly, stepping around a stray keg of rum. Had his idea been foolish? How much could the day school do for the slums, if the brightest boys could be spirited off to an almshouse and imprisoned there behind the fence until they were too old to be educated? That was the situation, and he had no control over it.

No control at all. He might as well try to control the ocean tide that pushed up the Avon River and flooded Bristol harbor. But the tide was God-created. And the almshouses!

"Mr. Conger, we can do something. We have to. We have to keep the children out of the almshouse. On the other side of that fence."

Conger did not turn his head. "But these children don't have parents. The almshouse feeds them. There isn't anything else to do with them, Mr. Müller."

George pumped his short legs to match step with Conger. Puffing a little, he said, "There is. Put them in orphanages."

Conger plodded along. "Orphanages! There aren't more than three orphan asylums in England. None in Bristol."

"There should be."

"You talk like a radical, Mr. Müller. Orphanages are an experiment. A pretty revolutionary experiment. I don't think we have any call to criticize the almshouses. They're established by law, been established for a hundred years and they've been proved—" He broke off. "Besides, how would an orphanage help your day school?"

"Don't forget," George said slowly, "it is the students we worry about before the school."

"I don't understand."

"Teach the children in orphanages instead of schools. How's that for an idea?"

"But there aren't any orphanages," Conger repeated stubbornly. He turned his back on the harbor and started uphill toward the city. Soon the smell of fresh sugar would be forgotten, and the city would taste like black dust in their mouths. As George turned reluctantly to follow him, he saw a schooner dip her sail and he was surprised to hear himself say, "Then I'll start my own."

"Mr. Müller! Start an orphanage! You couldn't!"

"Why not?"

"Why, sir, you don't have the time. You're the pastor of a church. And you have the day school already."

"Don't have time for boys like the little one with the big ears? Is that the only reason?"

"No. If you'll pardon me for saying this, Mr. Müller, you don't have the money either."

George sighed. Conger had thrown his last bit of mud at the enchantment of the docks. For he was right. George didn't have the money.

"So there's nothing you can do about the situation," Conger finished flatly.

But George had an answer before they were both swallowed up by the twilight of the filthy city. "Maybe not. But Conger, why did God put that thought into my mind?"

• • •

For the next month, thoughts about beginning his own orphanage tantalized George as he preached in Gideon Chapel and called on the sick. But at the same time, prosperous Bristol merchants and shipowners went on giving him their pounds for the day school, and George went on watching bright youngsters snatched out of classes and hustled away to the almshouse to be closeted with lunatics and criminals.

In January, Mary's missionary brother came home unexpectedly from the East Indies. Right away, he talked about going to Germany to recruit new missionary volunteers and he asked George to go along as interpreter. George had been away now for almost six years, and the thought of going home pushed the orphanage from his mind. On the first of February 1835, he and Groves sailed from Dover.

They docked at Calais, went directly to Paris, from there to Staatsburg, Germany, by fast mail coach, on to Stuttgart, and late in March rattled into the university town of Halle.

Dr. Tholuck was still there, teaching theology at the university. His house still smelled of coffee and mildewed books. The great mahogany table and chairs hadn't been moved an inch from under the dining-room chandelier. "This is great, Dr. Tholuck. It's good to talk German again. To hear you say, 'my boy.' It's been a long time. I feel like an old man."

Dr. Tholuck pulled George under the light. "Nonsense. You're not yet 30. But the father of two. How does it feel?"

George laughed. "Old."

"So we are all getting older. Maybe you won't recognize your friends in Halle. Schmidling has grown a beard—"

"Tholuck, I almost forgot. There is somebody here I promised I'd see. He's the son of a neighbor of my father. I wonder if you know him."

Tholuck did know him. He knew him quite well, and he knew also where George could find him. "Tomorrow, I take you to his rooms. He's living over at Franke's orphan asylum. The very floor where you lived. Now, what a coincidence!"

A coincidence? Had he come all the way back to Germany and to Halle to have Franke's orphanage thrust into his consciousness again? "O God, what are You trying to say to me?" was his heart's cry.

"My boy, you look pale. Come, we have coffee. And then we go over to the orphanage." George nodded. They would certainly go to the orphanage, and he would stand again in the room where he had lived as a new Christian. There he would pray quietly, asking for God's guidance in this thing.

In six weeks he returned to Bristol. But he came home to sadness. A chest and throat inflammation was plaguing the city, and when he had been home about a month his year-old son died.

At first, he punished himself. Had he spent too much time worrying over the underprivileged children and not enough time concentrating on his own? But could he have saved the boy? He was no doctor. And little Lydia was still healthy. In spite of the sadness in his own house, in spite of the torment, his work went on.

He preached twice on Sundays, shared a prayer meeting with Craik, and called on the sick, the aged, and the middle-aged lonely widows. There were always middle-aged lonely widows, and they always wanted him to linger over a cup of tea.

"Here, pastor, sit right down in my easy chair. And I'll get some tea. I always stop for tea. Now you will join me, won't you? Well—?" The woman hovered over the teacart, folding napkins with little mincing folds. "Now tell me, how's Mrs. Müller?"

"Quite well, this fall." George cleared his throat uneasily. To waste time on a woman with nothing more wrong than self-centered loneliness was sin. He should be out helping those who desperately needed real help. Inwardly, he seethed at this delay. "Would you like me to share some Scripture with you?"

"Over tea. So much cozier, don't you think? It's all ready in the kitchen. Now you just sit there and look at my books." The teacart jingled merrily out toward the kitchen.

Sighing, George edged forward in the overstuffed chair to read the titles of the books—Virgil, Cicero, Thackeray too. So she went in for the popular froth of the moment, exactly as he would expect. But what was this? From behind a leatherbound volume of poetry, a book slid off the shelf into his hand. It was the biography of Franke from Halle!

He stared down at it. He knew the book well.

Already he had read it twice, each time profoundly stirred by the faith of the man who had dared to go against eighteenth-century customs and build an orphanage. The man had had no money; he had simply asked God to send it to him, and God had.

Holding the book in his hand, George wondered how much it had influenced him to begin his own adventure with God. And now to meet it again, here in this widow's house. It was also more than coincidence.

He took tea with the widow on November 19, 1835. For the rest of the week, he thought about nothing else. At the end of the week, he went to Henry Craik's study, and he confided in him a plan that was now fully shaped in his own mind.

This was it: he would rent a cheap house right in the middle of Bristol. He would take any youngsters that needed a home, at least twenty or thirty, and feed them, clothe them, and educate them, as if they were his own family.

But Henry, fidgeting with a tatted doily on the chair arm, was discouraging. He said frankly that it would never work, and he gave his reasons. George had no money.

"Franke had no money either. He built his orphanages by prayer," George argued.

Henry's eyebrows lowered darkly. "Franke lived a hundred years ago."

Back and forth George stamped while the china vase on the mantel trembled. "What do you mean? God has lost His power?"

"No, no, George! But times are different."

"If God answered prayer in 1727 for Franke, He answers it in 1835 too. And I'll tell you something else, Henry Craik—to prove that is my real reason for starting an orphanage."

Henry looked disgusted. "But I thought it was the alms-house. The children."

George sat down on the sofa. "I'll be honest. The children are important. And the almshouses are bad. But there's another reason too. Listen to me, Henry. To people in trouble, I'm always saying, 'Trust God. Pray to Him. He will answer your prayer.' But it's hard to convince them."

"Quite." Henry agreed. "We live in a cynical age, old man."

"But I know you can reach up and touch God when you pray. I've proved it to myself. It changed my life. And I want to convince other people. I think I can if I can point to something God has done—through prayer. Something real and tangible."

"To show the whole world God answers prayer?" There was a skeptical note in Henry's voice. "That's why you'll build your orphanage?"

"No, no! For the children, of course. But for this reason also. If

God can take me, a very poor man; if I can bring together twenty children in an orphanage; if He will give me the strength to ask no man for anything—to ask only Him for my money—then I will prove to some people anyway that God is still faithful today."

"To ask nobody at all? Just to pray?"

"Yes."

Henry said nothing, fidgeting still with the tatted doily. On the sofa, George felt suddenly very much alone. But at the same time, he had never felt so sure that God was with him.

10

Open Thy Mouth Wide

I t was impossible to tell from the back of the women's bonnets and the men's starched collars how his Gideon Chapel
congregation had taken his news on that December 9, 1835. But
standing in the back of the chapel near the door, George knew
he had only to pronounce the benediction, and even before his
"Amen" had stopped echoing against the austere walls, the bonnets and the collars would rush down the aisle and he would no
longer wonder how they had reacted to the news that he would
add thirty Bristol orphans to his responsibility.

". . . and now in the name of the Father, the Son, and the Holy
Ghost, Amen."

The baker's wife reached him first. He had expected she
would. "Mr. Müller, orphanages are newfangled and downright
unhealthy."

His pudgy mouth like a lopsided doughnut, her husband, the baker, pushed along behind her. "Wife's right. Almshouse is good enough for street urchins."

George tried to shake hands as if these people were making perfunctory remarks about the weather. "You're mighty young to set yourself up against what's tried and true." The next woman shook her finger in his face.

"Thirty years old, and pretending you know so much!" The grocer, the clerk, the shopkeeper shuffled by. "We got along fine in Bristol before you lived here."

"Looks to me like a harebrained scheme. Plunging in without any thought, that's what you're doing."

That was unfair. George had thought about this, had prayed about it for weeks. He had not called this special meeting to announce his plans until he was sure he knew what God wanted. Isolating himself in his study, away from Mary and Lydia and the homely noises of cooking and dressing and playing, every day for weeks he had prayed the same daring prayer:

"God, I need a thousand pounds to get started. I need to find a house that's big enough for a family with thirty children. I need at least three or four for my staff, Christian folks that like children and know how to teach them or cook for them or manage them. And the children will need clothes and beds to sleep on and dishes to eat from. I believe You can do it, and I'll leave it all right in Your hands. Amen."

Each day after he had prayed, he wondered if he was being

too bold. Was he asking for too much this time? Then one day he opened his Bible and, as he often did when he was puzzled or lonely or waiting for God to speak, he read a psalm. He started with 79, read 80 too, and began the next one.

"Open thy mouth wide, and I will fill it." He read verse 10, and he almost laughed out loud. That was his answer! He had opened his mouth wide, wide enough to ask God point-blank for a list of tangible needs. And God had not rebuked him. There it was in the Psalms, and he believed with all his heart God was talking to him. "Open thy mouth wide, and I will fill it." It was a promise; now he was ready to stake his dreams on it.

The congregation were still coming down the aisle, some edging along close to the other wall and out of the door without speaking. One bonnet bobbed in front of him, and he reached out to grasp a warm hand.

"God love you, Pastor Müller," a butter-soft voice said. "Why didn't you take up a collection?"

Open thy mouth wide, and I will fill it! "No collection, sister. That was my bargain with God. I'll ask no man."

"All the same, here's my bit. 'Tisn't much. Just 10 shillings. But it's a start."

"God bless you, sister." The bonnet bobbed on.

"Pastor Müller, I'm able-bodied and I can sew and—" A square-shouldered woman braced herself in front of him. "I know I don't look stylish, but I can cook up good dumplings, and I get along just dandy with children. Can you use me, Pastor Müller?"

Open thy mouth wide, and I will fill it. "Use you? Why I—God bless you."

"I wouldn't take no pay." The shoulders seemed to get squarer and broader. "Just bring my little pension along with me and trust the good God for the rest."

There was only one answer to give her. "Open your mouth wide, and I will fill it." The next man in line looked puzzled, but George pumped his hand, and beaming, reached out for the next.

But one thing tarnished the shiny wonder of it all. That was Mary. Mary was dubious. She doubted, she was pessimistic. She was also cross.

"Don't throw that envelope on my clean kitchen floor," she snapped at George the morning after the public meeting.

But, skimming his letter, he hardly heard. "This is great, Mary. Great! I just announced it yesterday and already—"

From the pantry, a fury of rattled dishes. "Already your homeless children want to move in?" Mary called out.

He ignored her. "It's a letter from a husband and wife, a Christian couple—"

"Who?"

"Nobody we know. From up country. But listen."

He began to read, raising his voice to reach around the corner of the pantry door. "'We propose ourselves for the service of the intended Orphan House, if you think us qualified for it.'"

The fury of the dishes diminished, then mounted. "Oh?"

"That's not all. 'Also to give up all the furniture which the Lord has given us. For the use of your home!'"

Mary peered around the pantry door, her hands in the flour. "All their furniture!"

"'. . . and to do this without receiving any salary whatever, believing that if it be the will of the Lord to employ us, He will supply all our needs.'"

"But they don't even know you, George."

"We know the same Christ. That's enough."

"Two helpers already. Just like that. In one day." She came out and stood by the range. "In one day!"

"Three helpers. You're forgetting the woman that makes dumplings."

"Three helpers and a houseful of furniture."

"And 10 shillings."

"So soon. You didn't ask anybody, did you, George?"

"No one," George told her solemnly.

"It must—there's only one thing to think. God wants it that way."

He wanted to hug her. But instead he said casually, "Of course He does. Believe with me, Mary."

She fingered the frying pan on the range. At last she said, "I think I can."

"Thank God!"

"Yes, let's thank God. Right here in my kitchen." She closed her eyes, leaning against the range. "Dear God, take our little faith and make it strong. Give us what we need. Money and clothes and kitchen things and—so many things. We ask You for it. You are able. Amen."

They were standing there smiling at each other, George suddenly grateful he had married this sensible English woman, when they heard the banging on the back door.

At the door stood a man he had never seen before; only the tip of a wind-red nose and two teary eyes showed over the stack of bundles in his arms. "For your orphans," a voice squeaked from behind the stack. Down on the floor went the bundles, and the man was back on the pavement and scurrying up Paul Street before George could say a thing.

Mary was in the doorway behind him. "Well, open them!"

The frayed string snapped easily. They tore at the wrapping paper, both squatting together on the kitchen floor. Inside the wrappings were half a dozen bumpy bundles tide up in more crumpled dirty paper.

The wrapping fell away from the first one. "Dinner plates!" Mary exclaimed. "Twenty-eight dinner plates. Enough for—"

"Twenty-eight dinners for twenty-eight people."

"And here are three big serving dishes."

"Three wash basins."

Mary grabbed at the next bundle. "A jug."

George was tugging at the wrappings. "Drinking mugs. Three salt stands."

"A grater." Mary triumphantly set it on the floor. "And four knives."

"And five forks." George waved them in the air. There on the kitchen floor, in front of the range, the plates and dishes and mugs and salt stands stood in the old wrapping paper. From nowhere at all, a stranger had brought what the orphanage would need right to their door. How did this man with the squeaky voice know they had prayed that morning for kitchen things? George was sure he would never really know, but he was also sure that he had an answer that was good enough for both Mary and himself.

And the month that followed convinced him. That very week, a Bristol businessman gave him fifty pounds, intended for the orphanage.

"Fifty pounds," Mary said. "We lived for a year on fifty pounds when we got married."

They prayed for clothes for thirty children. Someone donated twenty-nine yards of sturdy material. They prayed for more helpers. A housekeeper volunteered.

A week later, a Bristol merchant, who had shown considerable irritation at George's preaching, came to the house with one hundred pounds, designated for the orphanage.

And late in January, George came into the kitchen, took the meat pie from Mary's hands, set it on the table and, grabbing her by the waist, whirled her around and around.

"I have it," he said, "I have it!"

"The house?"

"Yes, the house. A Wilson Street monstrosity. A lonely old monstrosity standing there, just aching to have thirty children move right in and slide down the banisters and shout from the attic to the back pantry, and even write on the walls. It's an ark, Mary, but it's so homey, you have to love it."

"What about the kitchen?" Mary asked practically.

"Big. The range looks good. And the oven! Wait till you see the oven."

"And it's really yours?"

"All mine, and all ready to move into on February 1. Mary, we've got our orphanage. We've got everything we need."

"Except the children." They stood there, beaming at each other. "Isn't God good, Mary?"

"He is. Now, you give me back my meat pie, and we can eat."

• • •

From the outside, the brick house on Wilson Street, lined up flush with the pavement, looked no different from its neighbors. Its six prim windows facing the street were spaced exactly like the windows in the house next door, exactly like the windows in the house next to that. The whole street resembled a line of not-very-bright school children in uniform. Steps that were nothing more than the way to go from pavement to door decorated the house, and identical steps led to all the houses on parade down Wilson Street. But as George swung open the door to 6 Wilson Street on the morning of February 3, he knew that it was different. From that day on there wouldn't be a house like it on the street, nor in Bristol, nor anywhere in England.

He sat down at a small table in the front room. The doors of 6 Wilson Street were now officially open. Anybody could walk in and make application for a homeless child. February 3 had been announced as opening day and, as George spread out papers and account books, he was confident that the room might be so crowded with applicants that he would have to ask some to wait in the kitchen.

He hoped not because the kitchen had not yet been repainted.

For half an hour he sat and daydreamed about painting the kitchen and rearranging the furniture in the dormitory bedrooms. After a while, he walked over to the front door and peered out through the small window. An open door would look more friendly, but this was February. He hesitated, then went back to the table. For an hour he concentrated on the bookkeeping, and then he began to feel uneasy.

At the window, he looked up and down Wilson Street. A crooked old woman shuffled along, peered up at the house curiously. He wanted to rap on the window to her, but she went right by. When she stopped a well-dressed man coming along the street, he realized she had been a beggar. The well-dressed man went right past too.

Now he was feeling hungry. It was almost noon. There was nothing in the kitchen to eat; he had been too excited to plan for food. Aimlessly he picked up his pen and began to add up columns. It was very still except for the popping of old beams in the cold and the coughing of his pen.

He walked to the window again. Outside, the gray houses marched on down the gray street, like so many children who had forgotten to wash their faces. A few snowflakes spit against the window, and the people who had been on the street had all gone home.

Then he had to admit the terrible truth. Nobody was coming. No city officials. No grateful aunts and uncles. No wistful, shivering children. Not even any irate almshouse authorities. Nobody at all. Nobody was coming.

He could hear the baker's wife and her friends. "Didn't we tell you? Doesn't this prove it? Bristol isn't ready for a newfangled orphanage yet."

He faced the waiting banisters in the front hall. "I don't know. I just don't know," he said out loud. But no one opened the front door to answer him.

11

Silverware, Pictures, and Furniture

Nobody?" Mary looked up at him as if she were going to cry. She sat on the parlor floor, surrounded by bolts of flannel and calico. He saw at a glance that she had been cutting out dresses for the little girls to wear. She looked like a forlorn child herself, asking him again, "Nobody at all, George? Are you sure?"

"Nobody came near 6 Wilson Street. Not a child. Not a grandmother. Not a city official. Nobody."

"Nobody applied?" she repeated dully, rolling the bolt of flannel back and forth on the rug. "Where were they?"

The drabness of the parlor, the pitifulness of her evenings spent over the cheap flannel, all that they had sacrificed—it was overwhelming. "Maybe we better ask ourselves—where was God?" he retorted.

Mary's eyes widened in horror.

"All right, where was He?" George persisted, flogging himself as well as Mary with the torturous thought. Then suddenly, he wanted to throw himself down beside the chair and beat it with his fist until the stuffing wheezed out, and cry out to God. "Mary, Mary," he said.

"Oh, George!" She pushed the flannel away and got to her feet.

"All the way home from Wilson Street, I've been praying. God, where did I fail? 'Open thy mouth wide, and I will fill it.' That's what He said, I believed He would."

"He did. George, He did. Until—"

"Yes. I prayed for money." There were both bitterness and sadness in his voice. "He sent gifts larger than I dreamed about. From people I didn't know."

"I prayed for kitchen things—"

"—and a strange man came to the door with his arms full. I know, Mary. We prayed for cooks and teachers—"

"—and they came. You prayed for clothes and got them. You prayed for—" She stopped suddenly, her eyes widening. "Oh, George!"

He was too preoccupied with his tragedy to see that her eyes were sparkling. "I believed He would go on giving me what I prayed for. I believed that, Mary. Until today."

"George, George, that's it!"

What ailed the woman? There was a joyous lilt to her words that made no sense at all. "That's it," she said again. "Everything you prayed for."

"Don't you understand what's happened, Mary? He gave me everything I prayed for, all right. Except children."

She looked as if she wanted to laugh. "That's it. You didn't ask for children."

"Didn't ask for—" What was she saying?

"Well, did you? I didn't. We never prayed together for them. Did you, George?"

He suddenly felt weak, as if he had awakened from a terrifying dream. She was right. They had prayed for everything—everything from plates to underwear. But they hadn't asked God to send the orphans.

"Don't you see, George? You thought—"

"There'd be too many."

"So you didn't."

"I didn't. Mary, I didn't." Now he wanted to laugh and take his wife in his arms and kiss her and praise God all at the same time.

"George, aren't we stupid?"

"Terribly stupid."

"And isn't He an incredible God!"

What they did next was the only logical thing to do, in George's mind. There in the parlor, they bowed their heads and in a few simple sentences made the request they had forgotten. They asked God for orphans and then, after Mary had picked up the flannels and all the parts of the little girls' dresses, they went out to the kitchen and had their supper of lamb stew. George could not remember when lamb stew had tasted so good.

The next morning, he woke full of confidence. At breakfast he told Mary not to expect him for lunch, trying to sound casual.

But the spoonful of porridge meant for little Lydia stopped in midair. "Won't be home? Where'll you be?"

"Over at 6 Wilson. Where did you expect?"

"Not today. What do you expect!" She stood there, frowning, shaking her head. But he got up, patted her arm, tugged Lydia's hair affectionately, and quickly went out the back door.

At 6 Wilson the key stuck in the lock, and he was twisting and jiggling it when he realized that there were two people on the pavement, watching him curiously. One was a young woman, whose bonnet perched like a giant pink bird on a nest of frizzy yellow straw. Every once in a while, she reached out to cuff the 10-year-old boy whose grimy shirt matched his face.

"About time," he heard the young woman say. "Come here, stupid. Drop it, I say. Don't go tossing rocks around here. Now mind."

George forgot his key. "Are you talking to me?"

"Sure, who else?" The young woman fluffed up the yellow curls. "Oh, and him too. The cross-eyed brat. Hey, this 6 Wilson?"

He pointed to the number above the door, and she nodded, shoving the boy ahead of her. "Well, we're here then. You the Reverend that's running this place?"

It seemed an hour before the key finally found the right notch, and the door swung open. The young woman minced into the parlor ahead of him, and he saw her eyes putting price tags on the curtains and the rugs. "Pretty swell place."

He showed her into the parlor, pulled up a chair for her, and sat down at the little table where he had waited alone the day before. The boy was already halfway out to the kitchen. "Hey, put that rock down, you hear!"

Briefly, the young woman told him her story. Jerry was her sister's boy. The sister had died. As for the father—she arched her eyebrows and shrugged, and the pink bird bobbed and almost took flight. She said she had planned to bring the boy down yesterday, but her gentleman friend had gotten a bit of a holiday from the docks.

"I'm sorry you didn't come yesterday," George said gently.

"You mean I'm too late? Of all the rotten luck. I told him—"

George was tempted. "Not quite too late. There are still a few vacancies." But he couldn't lie about it. "Madam," he said, "you are the first applicant and I'm delighted to see you."

Suddenly, a sharp pain pierced his big toe. He looked down. Jerry, grinning at him, had dropped the rock.

"Don't mind him," the young woman said. "He's good. Down in his heart. If you can find it." George wanted to take off his shoe and limp around the room in agony. But he stayed behind the little table. "Hey, you say I'm the first that applied?"

He managed to nod.

"Well, it don't look like I'm the last."

Coming through the door were a half-dozen women, of assorted ages and sizes and accents. With them were twice as many children, and everybody was chattering at once. They swept down on the little table. "Are you Mr. Müller?" "Pardon me, young man, where can I find the Reverend?" "Hey, is this the asylum?"

But over their heads, George saw what was about to happen even before he heard the crash. Jerry had picked up his rock, and had proclaimed himself leader of all the orphans with one single gesture. He hurled the rock through the parlor window.

"My window!" George said helplessly.

Immediately the pink bonnet bobbed up and down furiously. "Now don't get in a huff, Reverend. You asked for these kids, didn't you? Well, you got what you asked for, so don't complain none."

Within a month, applications for forty-two children had been filed. And in the spring, May 1836, the orphanage at 6 Wilson Street officially opened, and the children, the cooks, and the housemother moved in. Now George and Mary had forty-three children, counting 4-year-old Lydia, as their responsibility. And soon they heard of so many little babies who desperately needed a home that George rented a second house on Wilson Street. At the end of the year, he opened his second orphanage. And nine months after that, he rented a third house on the same street— and before anybody had time to repaint the parlors or polish the windows, thirty orphan boys from the Bristol slums were sliding down the banisters.

• • •

A year and a half went by. George kept his word; he never talked about money in public; he refused to ask anyone for a donation. But Bristol people gave regularly and generously to the three Homes. There was more than enough for food bills, staff salaries, clothing, and schoolbooks.

But two years after the first Home opened—on August 18, 1838—George was forced to write in his diary: "I have not one penny in hand for the orphans! In a day or two, many pounds will be needed!" He was terribly concerned. In Teignmouth, when the deacons forgot to empty the contributors' box, he had been responsible only for Mary. Now there were ninety-six orphans!

That day, he pleaded with God. "God, the Infants' Home needs ten pounds today. I've given them all that's in the treasury, but it was only five pounds. They need five pounds more, and they need it today. God, I'm trusting You to supply it, somehow."

The woman who fluttered into his home on Paul Street a little later was wearing a silk dress that rustled under her cape, and George sniffed perfume as she sat down in his study. But she reached a tiny, gloved hand into her purse, sighing confidentially, "So when God told me not to wear those glittering gaudy jewels anymore, Brother Müller, He told me something else too. He told me to get rid of them."

A tiny handful of coins tinkled on his desk. "And give the money to somebody. I thought of the orphans. Now I do intend to sell them, but it might not be for weeks, so I thought I'd come right here today with what they're worth."

His eyes sorted out the coins while she talked. "Actually those glittering gaudy jewels weren't worth very much, I'm afraid. The coins won't amount to much."

"Five pounds," George interrupted.

"Five pounds and a few shillings over. God doesn't give you much through me, but—"

"Not much. So much!"

"Just five pounds."

"More than five pounds. He gives the exact answer to prayer. Right down to the very pound!"

For the next two weeks money only trickled in. The house-mothers bought bread for one meal at a time. And on September 5, George faced serious trouble again. In his journal, he wrote, "Our hour of trial continues still. The Lord mercifully has given enough to supply our daily needs. But He gives by the day now, and almost by the hour, as we need it."

Now he ate his meals in discouraged silence. When Lydia wanted to play, he turned away. Yet doggedly, he held to his determination: he would prove that God hears and answers prayer. He would prove it, and all that it required was patience.

But Henry Craik thought differently. "George, you've worked yourself into a fine mess. All I suggest is a way out."

"Your way isn't God's way," George said stubbornly. "I won't ask anybody for money. What would that prove? I'll ask God, and that's all."

"But *Christian* friends are different. They're interested in this thing, old man. All you need to do is go to them and tell them how things are financially and—"

"No!" George exploded.

"But look here, fellow, you've got almost a hundred children to feed. You can't be irresponsible about this. It's rather like you were their father."

"'Father to the fatherless,'" George muttered. That was the verse he had counted on.

"Quite. How many times have you quoted that verse yourself?"

"Who is 'Father to the fatherless'? Not I. It's God in Heaven. 'Father to the fatherless.' He'll provide."

"Through channels, George," Henry prodded.

"He'll choose the channels. Not Müller. You'll see, Henry, He hasn't failed yet. I'll pray, and the money will come in."

Henry picked up his great coat from the sofa and buttoned it up carefully. Then he said clearly, "The money will come in. But it'll go out again, just as fast. And more will come in, and it will go out. And it's my wager someday it'll go out faster than it comes in." At the front door, he called back, "And then where will you be, George Müller?" The door closed behind him, and George was alone in the parlor, remembering his words.

But even Henry's pessimism could not turn him away from his bargain with God. He would not ask anybody for money, only God.

A little later, Brother Terrence, from the staff, walked into his study. On George's desk, he unloaded a pocketful of small coins.

Five people had stopped at the orphanage that morning, all to make donations. They had been small gifts, but they added up to something helpful.

George swept the money into his purse. The young staff member scowled. "Aren't you going to give me that money to use for the house? I've a bill due tomorrow and I—well, I thought, after all—"

George interrupted. "Tomorrow! 'Sufficient unto the day is the evil thereof.' Brother Terrence, today I prayed for this money to make up an overdue salary. God sent my answer by you. This money goes for that—today. Tomorrow we pray for your bill."

But the fear that Henry Craik had not been wrong nagged him. For the money did go out as fast as it came in. Every day he watched it happen, and at the end of the week—on September 10—George knew he must take drastic action.

The staff that drifted into the shadowy parlor of 6 Wilson Street on September 10 and huddled together on a ring of stiff little chairs were a gloomy bunch. It had rained all that day and the day before, and the house smelled of the wet clothes molding in the laundry room downstairs. Mingling with it were the fumes from a half-hearted soup boiling its goodness away in the kitchen.

George faced his staff with a pounding heart. For days now he had fought against what he was about to do. Call the staff together and tell them the truth? Say "We are down to nothing, and God sends help or else we close our doors"? How could he? Wasn't that the same as asking them for money, as asking men for money?

But it had been no mere rationalization that had brought him to this point, facing his staff in the Wilson Street parlor. Before God, he had seen the light. By not telling his own staff the state of affairs, he had been cheating them. He had been cheating them by not letting them pray with him and experience the excitement of God's answer. He had prayed alone, and he had told them about it, and they had used the money. But it wasn't the same. In a way, he had been cheating them.

So he was breaking no pact with God. He was renewing it by sharing it.

"Staff," he said, "I have something very sad and very wonderful to share with you." The small talk about head colds and gruel hushed, and they all waited for George Müller's next words.

He had not expected anything like their response. When he finished, one woman rose and faced him accusingly. "It might help matters a little to cut expenses."

"We've pared them to the bone, sister."

"No, you haven't. You forget one item."

"What's that?"

"My salary. My widow's pension is very adequate. No, Mr. Müller, I won't take another pound from you as long as I work for your orphanages."

Another staff member reached for his hand. "I'm on my way upstairs to pray," he said quietly. "But take this first." It was several pounds.

"I couldn't," George began.

"And I couldn't get on my knees and ask God for money while I was holding back the cash. Take it."

The little cook's lips were quivering but she blurted out, "Count on six pounds from me. It's my little nest egg up to the bank. But I'm sending for it directly. If you'll excuse me now, I'm going out to tend the soup, and get some praying done while it's simmering."

Well, he had done it. He had told his staff the truth about the money. He felt strangely sure that he had done right. But the rest was in God's hands. It was up to Him.

He smiled over the assortment of coins they had given. Enough to pay the baker and the grocer for a day or two, but not much else. Yet they had meant so well. Now, if they would pray.

By the end of the week, the pitifully small collection was gone too. And George noticed a strange uneasiness at the orphanage. When he tried to ask two of the staff to help him move a bookcase, they hurried past, out of the house, pretending they hadn't heard. In midafternoon, and with their arms full of bundles! When he called to the housemother, he saw her hustle out the back door. She too was carrying something.

That night, he ate his supper at the orphanage. After supper the young staff member who stuttered a little stood up to make a speech. After a few laborious sentences, he pushed an envelope down the table toward George. "... every tuppence for the orphans," he said.

In bewilderment, George took the envelope. "Where did this come from? You don't have any money. None of you."

"It's your answer to p-prayer. So the orphanage can stay open."

"I want to know where it came from." George was on his feet.

"It's an answer to prayer."

"I *will* know."

"We had some things we didn't need," somebody called up from the end of the table.

"Things?" George asked.

"In our rooms. Silverware, pictures, a little furniture."

"You sold them?"

"They were things we didn't need. That's all. After all," the young staff member blushed, "we didn't want you to have all the f-f-fun, Mr. Müller."

"Fun?" George asked, aghast.

"We wanted to have a hand in some answered prayer too."

But in a very few days, this too was all gone. Then for five terrible days God kept the orphanages from hour to hour. But on September 18, George knew he could go on no longer. The houses had been stripped of everything but their essentials. None of the staff members had a shilling left in the bank. The only resource was God.

And this was the last possible moment for God to step in and save George Müller's experiment.

He saw a woman pass in front of the parlor windows and wished in a moment of unreasonable irritation that strangers would not always peer into street-level windows. In his own home on Paul Street, the first floor was nicely above the sidewalk.

Then to his surprise, the woman he had noticed was inside the orphanage, fidgeting with an immense carryall as she crossed toward him.

"Well, Mr. Müller, they told me you were in your study, but I said to them, I've waited a long time to see you, and I didn't care if it was an imposition."

Like a gull exclaiming over a fish, she told him in short, excited sentences that she was visiting next door, and she had just come down from London for five days or so, and already the change of air was doing her the world of good. He caught her words. "We do like Bristol. So restful after London. Don't you think so, Mr. Müller? Nobody here ever worries."

Why should this nervous woman be added to his burden of the day? How could he stop the flood of words? "Would you like to look around the house?" he asked politely.

"Well, yes," she rattled on. "But before I do, I'll settle up my business with you. Well, it isn't really business. We don't like to think of it that way, do we? Now let's see. This purse of mine is all of a clutter. Ah, here it is." She laid on his desk some pounds, some shillings. He saw in a swift glance it was more than enough to pay the bills for a week, and perhaps if they were careful, two weeks.

"I would have been here before. I've been next door for five days."

"Five days!" She had been there all these last terrible five days. "But you were so busy. I kept peeking over. Meetings going on. Everybody looking so solemn. And then the other day, everybody rushed out carrying bundles. Picnic goodies, I suppose?"

"Not exactly." He resisted a hearty laugh.

"Dear me, I wish you'd explain it to me. All the busyness that goes on over here."

"My dear woman, you've explained our busyness to me."

"I don't understand."

"Madam, we've been busy these last five days—and three weeks—so God would make His answer to our prayers more wonderful. Take a chair, madam. I'll tell you the whole story."

12

A Big Bill Comes Due

He got through the next five years—1838 to 1843—by gritting his teeth and hanging on. If he thought about God's abundance as a great ocean, it sometimes seemed that the hand of the almighty Provider was willing only to squeeze out a few drops of His blessings at a time. At best, it was a meager trickle that got through to the bleak stone houses in the Bristol slums.

But grimly, George thought of his brushes with bankruptcy as ironic proof of the very thing he had set out to prove. Ironic, but nevertheless wonderful.

One November day, when his purse was flat again, he and his staff knelt in the Wilson Street parlor and told God frankly they were in trouble. After prayer, George got to his feet saying, "God will send help. I know it." He turned around and saw a letter lying on the little table. It had come in the post while they had been praying. Mary had slipped in quietly and laid it on the table. George ripped it open. It contained ten pounds, enough to cover expenses for at least a week!

Another day, the Boys' Home needed eight pennies to pay the grocer and the baker for dinner that night. There was no other food in the Home at all. But the Boys' Home counted only seven pennies in its till, one penny short. An emergency request went out to the Girls' Home. Was there anything in the contributors' box? The box was properly rattled. Yes, there certainly was. Then would they open the box? The lid was flipped back, and just a single coin tumbled out—a penny. Exactly what the Boys' Home needed for dinner, and nothing more!

"The ordering of our kind Father," George wrote in his diary that night, "who not in anger but for the trial of our faith keeps us poor."

One Saturday night there was no bread in any of the three houses for Sunday. A friend came to visit and, unaware of the state of the cupboards, handed George half a sovereign. The friend arrived at eight-thirty; the stores stayed open only until nine.

One disconsolate evening, George wrote in his diary, "Unless the Lord sends means before nine o'clock tomorrow morning, His name will be dishonored." At eight o'clock in the morning, a businessman stopped on his way to his office with 3 shillings. He had walked half a mile out of his way to come around by Wilson Street.

Time after time it happened like that. George wondered about the sense of humor of God in Heaven. It seemed like a peculiar way for God to build His monument.

• • •

"But that's the way He does it. A hundred orphans now in three Homes. And it's prayer that's feeding them, clothing them, and educating them. God has kept us for six and a half years now." The little birdlike woman, to whom George was talking, pursed her lips and nodded rapidly. They were standing in the hallway of the Paul Street house. It was November 1843. George lifted the little woman's coat from the hall tree.

"And tell your wife not to forget to bring down my shawl. I only have one, you know." She nodded again rapidly, her head jerking up and down as if it were on strings.

"We wish you'd take supper with us. It isn't every day we make a new Christian friend," George said, holding her coat.

"Mercy! Your tea was so stout I expect I won't have to buy my supper on the train! Supper? No thanks!"

It was the suddenly clear picture of this pathetic little woman huddled in some drafty coach, clutching her knitted carryall to her, going without supper, that made him say what he did. "The more responsibility I take on my shoulders, the more God supports. Now, Mrs. Brightman, I want to add you to my responsibility. I want you to share a common purse with me."

Her hand went to her mouth, and her watery eyes seemed about to overflow. "Why, Mr. Müller, whatever do you mean?"

"Now I've never said this to anybody but my wife—and the orphans. But I want you to feel that my purse is your purse. You've heard me tell today that it isn't a very thick purse. But we both share God's purse. Don't forget that. From now on, call on Mary and George Müller for any help. We have one purse together."

The woman looked frantic. "Oh, dear, oh, dear! What have I said?"

George smiled and patted her shoulder gently. "The one shawl. No supper on the way home. So many things."

"My dear young man—and you are very young—I didn't want to buy my supper because I'm afraid of indigestion. As for the shawl—Mr. Müller, there's something you don't understand. I've never had any money worries in my life. Just recently, I inherited a tidy little legacy. The legacy itself is worth five hundred pounds. You see, by most, I'm considered a rather wealthy woman!"

Later, after she had gone, with her shawl, and the knitted carry-all clutched to her, George tried to explain to Mary exactly what had happened.

"George, you insulted that poor woman!"

"Not poor," he said, ruefully.

"Well, what did you say to her after all that?" He had mumbled something about misunderstanding. And she had countered with the statement that she rather liked the idea of the common purse. But he had protested, insisted that under the circumstances she forget what he had said.

"I should hope so!" Mary said, pointedly. But the woman had said something else, something quite curious. She said that she thought the Lord had given her the legacy not as much for investment as for safekeeping. All this she had said standing with one hand on the doorknob in the Paul Street hallway.

"She has been praying about how to invest it, Mary," George concluded.

"George?" There was a worried question in Mary's voice.

"She wants me to pray too," he added hastily.

"Pray for what?"

George hoped he sounded casual. "Ask God to show her exactly where He'd have her put her legacy."

"George, you wouldn't."

But he already was. In the same room with Mary, he was already far away in a quiet place of his own, talking to his good Friend whose purse he shared. "Dear God," he prayed, "I bring to you the widow. Lord, make her so happy in Yourself that she knows her true wealth is only in You. Lord, show her the heavenly calling. Lord, make it so real, she'll want to lay all her gold at Your feet."

But the widow soon discovered that some of her best friends were dismayed about her trip to Bristol.

"I hope you didn't tell that cocky young fanatic you had any money," they said. And, "Don't tell me he offered to pray for you. How could you be so simple?"

And finally, "Please take our advice. Find yourself a good lawyer. Put that money in some sound investment that will earn money. Please, before it's too late." The little woman went on nodding her head, and thinking her own thoughts and remembering the Bristol orphanages.

A month went by. George went on praying. "Oh, Lord, it's almost a month! I've prayed faithfully for the widow every day. Twenty-four days. Work Your will in her life. I'll keep my promise. I won't speak a word of my needs. I won't ask any man or woman. But, Lord, show the widow the way. I do feel she'd be blessed a lot if she gave her money right over to the orphanage."

But he heard nothing from her. He began adding to his prayer, "There's that big bill due the first of the year. It would help, God, if—"

Late in November, he came home one day to find the widow having tea with Mary. Her head bobbing furiously, her birdlike nose quivering, she said, "Mr. Müller, I want to share a common purse with you after all. The Lord has told me to give up my money."

"Well, this is—" George began.

"A surprise to you," she finished for him. "I know."

He cleared his throat, not daring to look at Mary.

She went on, "But don't refuse it on that account. I know it's what the Lord wants. He wants the orphanage to have my legacy."

Still he couldn't look at Mary. "I'm grateful," he said. "Very thankful. A little overwhelmed. But I can't accept it."

Mary set the teapot down with a clatter.

"Young man!" the widow chirped.

"Not yet. I can't let you rush into this."

"But why?"

"Why? I don't know how to tell you. I guess it's just this: I'm

134

frightened by the power of prayer. And I can't take your money until you've had time to make sure it's what you ought to do. Take two weeks. Then if He still says so, the orphanage will accept your five hundred pounds."

Five hundred pounds! It would pay that big bill, or it would be living expenses for all three Homes for more than a year.

The big bill was due on December 31. Just before the middle of the month, George received the widow's letter:

"Since I last saw you, I haven't had the slightest doubt about what I ought to do. I've asked my heart if I'm really doing this unto Him. My heart assures me I am. I want you to have the money. I'll forward it soon."

George answered her. "Your letter finds me in peace. It doesn't surprise me. Dealing with God is a reality. Praise God for His wisdom that made me speak about sharing one purse."

But the next letter, the handwriting like gnarled tree branches, said: "Dear Mr. Müller: How I hesitate to tell you that there is some delay in my signing the money over to you. Probably it won't be paid in full until January."

On December 31, George, biting the end of his pen, wistful again about the Almighty's sense of humor, was able to write, "In reference to the delay, I rejoice. This gives you a good chance to be sure you're doing right."

Somehow the payment was scraped together. Yet the first of January went by, and still the widow had not transferred her money. George fought the nagging fears in his stomach. Every day in January, he waited for her letter. But the month went by. Still nothing. And February too.

On March 8, 1843, she wrote: "The money has now been legally transferred. You'll find it waiting for you at your banker in Bristol. Use it the way you want. But please, Mr. Müller, do spend a little of it on yourself and Mrs. Müller."

The orphanages had 500 pounds in the Bristol bank! It was a small fortune, more than George Müller had ever accumulated before. And almost immediately he thought of a very excellent way to spend it.

13

Another House

"M r. Müller, sir, you know 4 Wilson Street?"

From her tone of voice, George couldn't tell whether the housemother was in a thanks-be-to-God or a you-have-to-cane-Johnny mood. He answered casually "How could I miss it? It's been next door all these years." He detected a slight twitching of her lips. "Another broken window?" he asked.

"No, sir, nothing like that. They're going to move."

"And?"

"Said they'd give us first chance at their house. I told them thanks, and said it was out of—"

He could hardly believe what he was hearing. "You mean, we have first chance to rent that house next door?"

The housemother had pressed her lips into a downward arch. "Well, the Grahams said you might want another roomy place to start another Home. But I told them, it's a pity, but we've no money at all, and I'm sure Mr. Müller wouldn't be that crazy to start another place."

His mind reassuringly patted the 500 pounds cached away in the Bristol bank. He swung open the door to his study and beckoned toward it.

"Come in. Let's talk. I have a big surprise for you."

As George leaned back in his upholstered armchair behind his desk, and the housemother perched uncomfortably on the squeaky little rattan chair against the wall, a smile kept pulling at the corners of his mouth. He was bursting to talk about his big surprise. He was aching to tell everybody that the orphanages were wealthier than they'd ever dreamed of being and that it seemed as if finally—in March 1843—the dark days of shilling-pinching were gone forever. As he spilled out the good news, he delighted in the expressions on the housemother's face—unbelief, relief, thankfulness, joy!

"It's a miracle," she interrupted at last. "All this money at once. And the house next door coming up for rent."

"And the two women who volunteered last week. That's our staff for the new Home."

"Then it's all settled."

George leaned back in his armchair. "Wait a minute. Nothing's settled."

"But the money—"

"Not just—poof—like that. I don't do things that way. I'll pray about it. We'll all pray about it. As we always do. Is this the hand of God, sister? Does He really want us to have four orphanages in Bristol?"

The housemother threw up her hands. "I declare, I don't understand you, Mr. Müller."

But she had no chance to say more. Outside the study door there was a splintering, then a crash that sounded as if the very spires of Buckingham Palace had toppled over. Small boys whimpered. Housemothers and cooks scurried and blamed and scolded. "Now you've done it."

"Broke right in two."

Distracted, George wondered what had broken in two. The front door? Or a person? The boys were yelling now.

"Master Colin, you're due for a caning." So it was Colin. Immediately irate female fists rat-tatted on the door. George sighed. "We'll talk about this later. It looks like I have other business."

The 10-year-old boy that approached the desk head down did not seem to have broken himself in two. It must have been his opponent. He perched on the edge of the little rattan chair and squeaked it by wiggling. "What did you do this time, Colin?" George asked, pulling his mind from the money in the bank to discipline.

"Banisters. Slid down."

"But what broke?"

"The banisters." He swung his feet back and forth in misery, and the chair squeaked its sympathy.

"Broke the banisters? A thin fellow like you?"

Colin stuck out his lower lip. "Wasn't just me. About six of us. Made a kind of chain."

George tried to look stern. "Six is too many. Two at a time, that's the rule."

"I know."

Fleetingly George wondered why God had included discipline in his calling. His ministry should be renting houses and praying for money, not this kind of woman's work. Feeding a 10-year-old boy was so much less complex than disciplining him. "Colin, it's always the same story. When you get yourself into a scrape, it's six others too. Or ten. Why, Colin?"

"Dunno." Very low.

"You hide in a gang. Almost as if you're afraid to be alone." He knew so little about what went on in a boy's mind, but he grasped at this due. "Colin, tell me, are you lonesome?"

Colin swung his legs furiously. Then he answered, "If my cousin was here, I wouldn't be."

"Who's your cousin?"

"Roggie Pitts. He wanted to come in too. You wouldn't let him. You told Granny there wasn't room for him."

There it was, right there in the study with them. "This Roggie," George said slowly, "he's with your granny?"

Colin's scrawny face grew old and wary. "No more. He got took to the almshouse." Then he was ten years old again. "I bet he breaks more than banisters for 'em there."

So the disciplining was part of it, after all. "God, I thank You for this ten-year-old," George prayed silently. "Through him, You've given me the answer to the prayer I thought I hadn't had time to pray. That prayer about whether I should open a fourth Home. God, thank You for sending Colin to me today."

Aloud, he said, "Now, Colin, you won't tell anybody I didn't cane you after all?"

"No, sir!"

"Run along. I've some thinking I want to do. About your cousin, I'll tell you—and everybody else—about it at the next prayer meeting. Run along, and don't get lonesome again for a while, please, Colin."

How could it have been made more concrete to him? Every day he was sending a dozen, a hundred, a thousand Bristol children to the almshouse by having no room for them. The more room he had, the more children he could save.

Yet although the parade of skinny children shuffling off to the almshouses haunted him for days, it wasn't quite enough. He wasn't ready to go next door and tell the Grahams he wanted first chance to rent their house. The first week he did a lot of peering over at it, sizing up the rooms by the shape of their windows, wondering about paint, or whether the third floor was big enough for a dormitory. The second week he figured a great deal on paper. The third week he went about his routine work as if he were listening for a voice.

And all this time he was praying. As he paced in the scrap of garden behind his Paul Street house, he argued with himself.

Was this the right way to spend the widow's money? Could he be sure? And one day he found that he had more than his own thoughts for debate. Henry Craik had slipped in through the garden gate and had something to say.

"Don't see what pleasure you get out of walking in this garden, George. You hardly wait till the snow melts. Tramping around in all that mud. What does Mary say about your shoes?" Henry's eyebrows slid up.

"Best place in Bristol for pacing." George ignored the pessimism. "And praying. The mud reminds me of the Devil." He pulled one shoe out of the clay, looked at it ruefully, and then set it back deeper into the spring mud.

"Well, George," Henry sat down gingerly on a garden bench leaning against the only tree in the garden, "you pace back and forth. But you still haven't decided. Why, old man, the house jolly well may have slipped through your fingers."

"Nonsense!" George sat down on the bench with him and, with a long twig, started scraping the mud from his boots.

"I think you *have* decided," Henry went on. "Decided you don't want that other house. And decided that the whole experiment is a mistake, and the sooner you retrench the better. But you won't admit it."

"That's not so."

"Then what are you waiting for? Not for want of children, that's sure. Bristol is full of them."

"Henry, I'm waiting for a sign from God."

"I wonder." Henry settled back and folded his arms. "I think you're tired of this business of hazardous living. I think five years of it was enough, and now you've got a little money in the bank—"

George flung down his twig, and the mud splashed up. "Aha! I have my sign."

"What are you talking about? I didn't see any bolt of lightning."

"You are the sign. Tired of depending on God, am I? Sick of my project? Want to toss over the orphanage? So that's what it looks like to you? Maybe it looks that way to everybody. Then I'll rent the house on Wilson Street and prove we survived seven years of trials, and we can survive more if we have to!"

"Don't be rash, old man. I only meant—"

"I have decided, Henry. It's for Colin's cousin and the rest, yes. But it's for the sneering skeptics too. Why, if I don't rent that house, it could disprove the thing I want to prove. It could say to people, I think God is faithful today, but not very much!"

He got up and tramped toward his house, and the mud sprayed up as he walked, and, for a moment, looked golden and pink in the light from the sun setting over the Bristol roofs.

The next day, he crossed over to 4 Wilson Street. Mr. Graham was irritable. "But, Mr. Müller, that was a month ago I spoke to your housemother. A full month ago."

"Just twenty-two days."

"I wish you had come sooner. We've changed our minds. We aren't going to move." They had looked, Mr. Graham and his daughter, but they hadn't found a place that was suitable. He was sorry to disappoint the Homes, but that was that.

"You aren't going to look any more?"

"There's one week left before we have to decide. We may look some. But I don't hold out any hope, Mr. Müller. I don't think we'll find anything suitable in Bristol. Come back in a week, and I'll let you know. But don't bother me before that. I know your persistent ways."

George left 4 Wilson Street defeated and wondering. "God, if You want this Home for Colin's cousin, and the rest," he prayed. "If You want to prove how faithful You are, then You'll find this crotchety old fellow a place to live. And it has to be this week, God!"

Where Mr. Graham went that week, George never knew. From behind the curtains at No. 6, he watched him start out each day, and he prayed. But once it began to rain before Mr. Graham was halfway down the block, and he came back. Although George peered at him closely every time he came and went, the expression on the old man's face never changed.

When George rapped at the door of No. 4 a week later, he had no inkling of the decision. He could only breathe a last prayer. "God, I put all in Your hands—the orphans and the folks who think George Müller is getting sick of his adventure with You."

"Ah, Mr. Müller, come in, come in!" Mr. Graham was smiling. "I thought you'd be over before this."

"You said a week."

"So I did. Come in, come in!"

"First, I must know. What about the house?"

"Mr. Müller, we found just what we were looking for. There's even a room on the third floor with a skylight. For Nettie's needlework, you know. We're moving just as soon as we can get out."

In the summer, number 4 Wilson Street became the fourth house for parentless children. One hot July day, they swarmed up the sidewalk and in through the big oak door.

Two little redheaded girls carrying dolls.

A boy with a face smeared with freckles.

A boy who blew a toy trumpet all the way.

Two more who pummeled each other right up to the door and into the house.

One little girl with a cold.

And Colin and his cousin, Roggie Pitts, who ran right through the door and up the stairs and then swished down the banisters screaming all the way. "Hey, there, bully banisters! Bully banisters, Mr. Müller!"

At the door, George shooed them all in, his mouth quirking up at the corners from sheer joy. Things had never looked so good for his experiment in prayer.

All went along smoothly for about two years.

Contributions came in regularly. Trouble over bills seemed like a thing of the past, and the new staff members heard about it only as if it were something that had happened before Queen Victoria's reign.

George went on praying for every financial need. There were now almost a hundred and fifty orphans who depended on him every day for food and clothes. He was still copastor at Gideon Chapel, and the Scriptural Knowledge Institute was still conducting its day schools in the slums and distributing Bibles to people who couldn't pay for them.

But one October day, in 1844, in a musty house on Wilson Street, a man slammed his kitchen door and exclaimed to a woman who was taking a knife to the potatoes as if they were a dangerous enemy. "Confound them brats, Bessie! They did it again."

The knife slashed the skin bitterly. "Another window, Pa?"

"Not just a window. The skylight." He sank down in the kitchen chair.

"You oughta get the law 'n order after them brats," she said in a monotone. "Third thing they busted in three months."

"They've ruined the street. Make so much racket a body can't sleep afternoons," he said. "Well, they asked for it, and they're gonna get it," he said, hoisting himself out of the chair.

"What you going to do, Pa?" she said. A potato peel flicked to the floor, and she shoved it out of the way with her foot.

"Write a letter."

"To the law 'n order?"

"Naw. Better than that. To Müller himself."

She slammed down the pot on the stove and, without looking up, said between her teeth, "That won't do no good. Letters won't touch that stubborn German preacher."

"This one will." The man stamped on through to the living room. He tossed back over his shoulder, "I'm gonna say, either he gets out and closes up every single one of them Wilson Street places, or else I'll find a way to get them closed up. You come here, Bessie, and find my pen."

14

So Many Miracles

B ut that's hateful, Daddy. A little noise never hurt anybody."
Thirteen-year-old Lydia Müller tossed a stone down into
the gorge. It was a game they always played when George and
his daughter walked along the banks of the Avon River, a contest
to see how many stones tangled with the brush on the gorge's
side and how many plunked into the stream that cut the city in
two. Today George was in no mood for games. The letter from
his Wilson Street neighbor was heavier in his pocket than a
basketful of stones. He was shocked by his neighbor's demand,
hurt, and tense over what would happen if he granted it.

The river below, always shining like a foreign coin and whis-
pering about lands halfway across the world, seemed smelly
and barge-choked today. But he was not sorry that Lydia had
tagged along. She was a good listener, this daughter that looked

so much like him with her solemn thin face and straight mouth with its turned-up corners.

Without thinking about it, he stooped for a stone and turned it over and over in his hand. "No, Lydia, these people have their rights. You forget, Paul Street is a long way from the noise. It would make my head ache to live next door to it. There are other things, besides the noise. The drains clog up every winter. We have too many people living in our Homes. It affects the water up and down the street."

"I don't know about drains." Lydia made a face and flung stones into the gorge in rapid succession. "But I know this. I think those people are hateful, but I don't really care. I never liked Wilson Street. It's ugly. When I was little and you used to take me over there every day, I wanted to cry. All those houses lined up in a row on the sidewalk. If I were an orphan, I'd never want to live on Wilson Street." George looked at his daughter weighing stones, playing a game, carefree. Amused at her and not caring about her answer, he asked lightly, "Where would you want to live?"

Another stone fell into the gorge before she answered. Then she waved her hands in a vague wide gesture toward the north and chalky treeless Downs on the edge of the city. "Oh, Daddy," she said, "I'd want to live in a wide-open place with lots of breeze! A place where you can smell the sea once in a while. A place with fields for playing. Daddy, that's why I'm glad about Wilson Street."

Her exuberance pulled his mind from his problem. "Why's that?"

"Because *that's* the kind of place we'll all live in when you move the Homes. A wide-open place with lots of breeze!"

Below them, the barges were getting thicker. They had almost reached the spot where the Avon widened to form the great harbor. They stopped, as they always did at this spot, to stare down, fascinated. "Lydia, Lydia, living with your father has turned you into an impractical dreamer. Don't you know, girl, we'll thank God if He finds houses in the slums for us?"

She turned to him, and her eyes were dreaming. "If God gave us so much already, why won't He give us a little more? This wide-open place, I mean?"

"All right, suppose He did. What would we do with it?"

"Build a Home," she said simply. "See, I'm not impractical. Look, Daddy, that ship's flying a Spanish flag. Maybe they're pirates."

She was his daughter, all right. Her mind skittering off to strange exotic lands, her implicit faith that God managed her affairs with as much attention as He had managed Elijah's. She was his daughter, and he supposed he had taught her. Suddenly, he realized what she had said. "Build houses!" Maybe she was teaching *him?* Not rent, but *build* a Home? In an instant his mind had constructed an immense brick dormitory—the kitchen in the most convenient location, enough rooms to isolate head colds and fevers properly, adequate laundry rooms, and in the back, a quiet study. All in a wide-open place.

"Build an orphanage," he said out loud. "Why, of course. Bless you, Lydia. You're not impractical. You're just George Müller's daughter."

He found an egg-sized stone then, and hurled it out over the rocky palisades. He stood there listening, and then presently he heard the plunk and splash that told him his effort was rewarded.

That night he knelt in his room and prayed his boldest prayer. "Now God," he said, "we have to get out of Wilson Street. 'Do unto your neighbor'—You taught that Yourself. We can close up completely, and I know You wouldn't want that. Or we can find another place in the slums, and that's not very good either. Or we can find a wide-open place and build our own orphanage, tailored exactly to our needs. So God, I put it right in Your hands. I need to find about seven acres here in Bristol, on a hill if possible. Then I need a contractor to build a place for—say three hundred children. And I need ten thousand pounds, at least."

He prayed the same prayer morning and night for thirty-six days. Sometimes he prayed it as he cut across town to the chapel from his Paul Street house. Sometimes he prayed it when Mary thought he was listening to her. The pressure to leave Wilson Street became stronger.

But on the thirty-sixth day—December 10, 1845—it happened. "George, it's one thousand pounds! Right in this envelope! How can you be so calm? The most money we've ever seen at once. A thousand pounds! George Müller, how can you be so calm?"

"I'm calm because I prayed for it. I asked God." It was true.

He felt no relief, certainly no surprise.

Mary sniffed, "Well, we prayed a good long time. A whole month."

"Thirty-six days this morning. What's that in God's sight? I asked for a sign that we should build, and I knew I'd get it."

Now he could be certain that God would send the rest. But it would mean more praying. More waiting. The wide-open place was still a dream in a 13-year-old girl's eyes. The plan to build his own Homes was still nothing more than colossal nerve. Four days later, Mary's sister came home from a London vacation.

Even before breakfast, she was at 21 Paul Street to talk about her trip. It was a cold morning, and George was hungry. He was much more interested in hot porridge than his wife's sister's warmed-over trip to London. "Sugar, please. And another bowl of porridge," he asked, knowing that he sounded cross.

Mary set the porridge bowl in front of him absently, while her sister chattered on. "I was there about three days altogether, you know, and—"

"Milk," George interrupted, his mouth full. Mary frowned.

"And the last afternoon I went to a prayer meeting, and that's where I met this man who had read your book about the orphanages, George, and he said he was very interested in the orphans. So I told him you were going to build—"

He gulped down the porridge. "Praying about building." The woman never got anything straight.

She rushed right on. "Oh, I forgot to say, this man is an architect and he said he'd help you." She stood back from the table, her hands on her hips, a satisfied smile on her face. "Well, George, this man said he'd build your orphanage for you."

Before he spoke, he thanked God, over the porridge. "Thank You, God, for taking my boldness in Your stride and giving me what I asked for in a way I never dreamed of." But he had to be sure. "He'll come out to Bristol and superintend the whole construction and won't charge a penny," his sister-in-law went on.

He interrupted. "One question. You forgot something important. Is this architect a Christian man?"

Her hands still on her hips, Mary's sister bounced up and down in exasperation. "Now, George, don't be stuffy." She turned away from the table, crossed over to the stove, flinging back over her shoulder, "Of course, he is."

Two more months went by. Donations trickled in, and the Building Fund grew slowly. Then, on February 2, 1846, he heard about the land for sale on Ashley Down. It sounded suitable; there were about seven acres.

The next day, puffing a little in the February wind, he walked out to the Down. The farther he got from town and the harbor, the fewer houses there were. The Down was orphan-lonely, aloof, treeless upland unloved by the rest of Bristol. He scuffed at the ground; he was standing, he knew, on a giant mound of white chalk. Far off he could see the city, but he could not hear boats or trains or harried people.

Seven acres, from there to there. Room to build here. But how could he be sure that this was what God wanted? Suddenly, he found himself remembering Devon, and then he realized that for the first time in months he was smelling the sea. Down in the hollow of Bristol, especially on the wharves, the saltiness was blurred by Spanish tobacco, West Indian rum, and filthy harbor water.

As he sniffed, he heard Lydia say as clearly as if she'd been standing there, "A wide open place with lots of breeze. A place where you can smell the sea once in a while. A place with fields for playing."

"Yes, God, I heard. Thank You! It will be Ashley Down—if I can pay the price," was the earnest response.

The next day, he started out to locate the owner of the land. He wasn't home. A maid said, off-handedly, that he might be back later, and Mr. Müller could stop around then if he had a mind to.

But George was in no mood for waiting until later. He rushed off to the owner's business office. When he arrived he was told that the gentleman had left minutes before.

Puzzled, disappointed, he debated with himself about his next move. Something told him that this disappointment had a purpose. Something warned him not to persist in finding the owner. Wait until tomorrow, it said. So George went home. All evening he knew that he had done the right thing.

The next morning he arrived at the owner's office early and found him at his desk. But the owner was not cordial. "Why didn't you come back last night, man?"

George started to explain, but he was interrupted. "I was expecting you. Wasted the whole evening expecting you. Don't mind telling you, nothing upsets me more than wasting time. Truth is, Müller, I hardly slept last night over this. Woke up at three. Awake until five. All the time heard a voice that said 'Sell Ashley Down to Müller.'"

"Sir!"

"Fact is, that plaguey voice said, 'Don't overcharge Müller. Don't even make a profit. Knock sixty pounds off every acre.' That's what it said. I'd been planning to make it one hundred-eighty pounds an acre. That'll bring it down to one hundred-twenty pounds. But if you had come back last night, Müller, the way you should have, that voice wouldn't have plagued me."

"I don't expect it would have." Rapidly George figured. Seven acres now would cost him only 840 pounds. At that rate, he could buy the land. But at the original price, it would have totaled almost 1,300 pounds, over his budget. "How can I thank you, sir?"

"Don't. Just pay me promptly. Pay me promptly for seven acres, and don't pester me again."

So George had his land and his architect. Within six months he had more than 11,000 pounds in the Building Fund. On July 5, 1847, ground was broken on Ashley Down. And two years after that all bills had been paid, 700 pounds were left in the fund, and the Home on Ashley Down was ready for its orphans.

On June 18, 1849, George and Mary stood on top of Ashley Down and watched them swarm up from the city. Three hundred orphans were marching all the way from the old Wilson Street

Homes up to the wide open Down, where a southeast breeze made the air as salty as the Devon coast! On they came toward the mammoth brick building that was going to be their new Home.

There were 120 old-timers from Wilson Street. And 180 new ones, recruited right out of the Bristol slums.

Little girls in their white capes and their poke bonnets.

Little boys in trim jackets, with their visored caps on their heads.

Big girls in white pinafores over dark blue skirts.

Big boys in long serge trousers.

On they came, toward George and Mary, past them into the new Home. George knew it was the most wonderful thing he had ever seen.

"I'll never forget the last three and a half years, Mary," he said.

"The miracle of the shillings and the pounds, that's what we ought to call it."

"So many miracles, Mary." They stood there quietly as the orphans filed by. The time the sovereigns came all wrapped up in a little brown paper package. The woman who told him to sell her gold chain, earrings, and a lovely gold brooch. The day that somebody sent 120 pounds, and while he was on his knees thanking God, the doorbell rang, and Mary took in a letter containing 200 pounds.

The last of the orphans—a little girl with a runny nose and hair the color of a sunset—disappeared through the door. "Well, Mary, there it is. Our orphanage and our orphans, all three hundred of them. It's all done now."

"Yes," Mary echoed, "it's all done now."

Before they could say more, the housemother burst out of the front door. "Oh, Mr. Müller, I looked all over for you! There can't none of us figure out those newfangled gas burners. Nobody but you knows how. And the water on the third floor too."

"We'd better go in, George," Mary said.

The housemother whipped around. "And Mrs. Müller, ma'am, the junior girls can't find their blouses nowhere. Do you suppose, ma'am?"

The corners of George's mouth twitched up, and then he started to laugh. He had been wrong. Yes, thank God that he was wrong.

"Wrong, George? What do you mean?"

"I said it was all done, Mary. But it isn't. It isn't all done yet. And do you know, I don't think it ever will be." Then he took her arm, and together they followed the housemother into the new orphanage.

15

Patiently Enduring

B ut a year and a half later, George Müller was restless again, not content with what he had accomplished. He began to think that God was telling him to expand the orphanages even more, and once he started dreaming about it, he couldn't stop.

The idea obsessed him night and day. Yet he didn't dare tell even Mary. Already, he was spending most of his days and most of his evenings on Ashley Down. Since the Home opened, he'd seen little of his family and less of the Gideon Chapel people. How could he handle still more responsibility?

But in December 1850, he made up his mind. He would triple the number of orphans and build a shelter for seven hundred!

When he confided his plans to a few, they said he was crazy. Especially his good friend, Henry Craik. Henry had his reasons. "You'll be way beyond your limit if you try to take on a thousand orphans." They were in the Visitor's Room at the Home, Henry pacing somberly along the bold-striped rug.

"Beyond my limit?" George asked from the chair in front of the gas fireplace. He crossed his leg and hooked a thumb between two jacket buttons, clutching the jacket's edge tightly with his wrist. In this pose, he was always ready for a battle.

"Beyond your limit spiritually!" Henry paced the stripes to the end of the room, then turned about and started back. "You know that verse: 'For I say, through the grace given unto me, to every man that is among you, not to think of himself more highly than he ought to think.' Old man, talk about asking God for another orphanage is spiritual cockiness!"

George clutched his jacket tighter. "You're wrong. God is sufficient—for anything. Look what we've survived already. And with every fresh trouble God has increased my faith. He'll go right on doing it. You're wrong, Henry. I haven't reached the limit of my spiritual measure."

"Then physically. George, there's a limit to a man's strength."

George relaxed his hand. The corners of his mouth turned up, and then he smiled broadly. "When I think that the German army turned me down, Henry! For sixteen years, I've carried on the management of these homes singlehanded. Look at me, I don't have an assistant. Every fifty-two weeks I write three thousand letters, alone."

"But there's a limit."

"And how can we say where it is? With the work still growing, I can't set a limit. Think of it, Henry! Fifteen years ago, we had just one Home. Thirteen, two Homes. Seven years ago, four rented Homes."

Henry's eyebrows raised and lowered in agitation.

"I know, I know."

"Five years ago, I dreamed about Ashley Down. And now, look at it! Henry, don't talk about limits to me."

"Then be practical. Where's the money coming from? For building, and upkeep? Well?"

George shifted uneasily in the straight-backed chair. "I've done some figuring. It'll take 35,000 pounds to build my next house. And it'll cost about 1,500 pounds for maintenance."

"Every year?" Henry shook his head.

"Every year. And God will give us that money as He gave us the baskets of bread twelve years ago on Wilson Street!"

"But you've got to stop somewhere."

"Suppose when we had our day schools and nothing else, we had stopped. There'd be nothing else today. But we didn't. Do you know what that means?"

"I have an idea," Henry said, wearily.

"Henry, six hundred orphans have been brought up and educated in the Homes. Several hundred thousand tracts have been distributed all over the world. Forty men are preaching the gospel all over the world, thanks to our Scriptural Knowledge Institute. And now we have a Home for three hundred orphans. And you think God is ready to *stop*?"

"You've made up your mind?" Henry asked gloomily.

"Of course I have. George Müller will keep right on working to bring more glory to the name of the Lord. That He may be looked at, magnified, admired, trusted in, and relied on at all times for everything. That's my goal, Henry Craik. And I'm going to build a bigger orphanage to reach it. A thousand orphans on Ashley Down, Henry. I won't stop until I have them." The corners of George's mouth went up, and he added, "I'm not entirely sure I'll stop then."

Yet he told no one about his decision for a long time. Even to confide in Mary he waited two months. It was a full four months after that when he made the public announcement that officially opened the Building Fund for the second Home on Ashley Down. He began now to pray that Christians would send him money earmarked especially "New Orphanage." It was all a matter of waiting to see whether Henry was right or wrong about the question of spiritual limits!

George announced his plan in May, and in August he was given 500 pounds, a sizable gift that promptly went into the Building Fund. A month later a valuable Coverdale English Bible, more than three hundred years old, was donated by an elderly gentleman.

But after the glorious start, money came in slowly. Somebody gave a handful of shillings; the next week, nobody gave anything. It went like that.

But it never occurred to George that God would not answer his prayers if he waited long enough and was patient enough. "After he had patiently endured, he obtained the promise." This was his verse through the rest of 1850 and into 1851.

It began to look as if he were going to need a great deal of patience. The Building Fund leveled off and stayed there. Three pounds, 14 shillings, two silver spoons, and two silver thimbles: this was a typical donation in the winter of 1851.

A year after he made the public announcement, he received a single gift of 999 pounds. Now he was sure God would build the Home.

A year later, he wasn't quite so sure. Three hundred and fifty orphans were already signed up for admission, but the fund had hovered at the same total for months.

Then somebody donated 8,100 pounds!

Now the money was coming in steadily, some large gifts, and some small. George and Mary and Lydia prayed on.

Four and a half years after George had confidentially told Henry he would triple the number of orphans on Ashley Down, in March 1855, he had enough money in his fund to talk about building. The new Home would be on Ashley Down, of course, a little to the northeast. One muddy day, he set out with a Bristol land agent.

The wind was blowing up from the sea that day, as fresh as spring in Devon, but it was apparent the land agent didn't care. His mind was on the mud underfoot. "Nasty business, hiking through this mud," he grunted, following George across the Ashley Down fields.

But George hardly heard him. He was intent on making a

dream come true. "Here we are," he explained and stopped short. "That's it."

"That's what?" asked the agent, shifting his clumsy record book from one hand to the other, and easing one foot out of the ooze.

"That lot right there. Begins down over there and runs right up to the orphanage. Check your records and see if I'm not right about the boundaries."

The agent balanced his book with one hand and leafed over the pages. He wet his finger and ran it down a column, muttering a little to himself. "Yes, yes, that's it, all right. There to there."

"Can't you see it now? It's brick like the first," George said, more to himself than to the agent. "But just a little bit gentler about the roof, I think. Not fancy. And a gable, just so. Six or eight gables, even, and for the front entrance, six small pillars. The rest is plain."

"What are you looking at?" the agent asked, twisting around.

"My new orphanage! What I'm planning to build on this lot, from there to there. For years, I've had my eye on it. I know just what it'll look like. But I had to wait until I had the money, you see, and—"

"Mr. Müller, I hate to disappoint you, but—"

George paused.

"Money won't do you any good."

"What do you mean? There's nothing built on it. See for yourself."

"Quite. But you can't build on it either, man."

"Why not?"

The agent pulled his foot out of the mud and looked at it sadly before he spoke. "Because of the owner," he said.

"Then I'll talk to the owner. Pray with him. Sir, do you realize I have seven hundred fifty orphans waiting to live in this Home? That there is space for less than four thousand orphans in all England? We must have this Home. I'll talk to this owner and—"

"That's impossible. The owner is dead!"

"Dead! But—then what's the trouble?"

"Unfortunately for you, sir, the owner left a will. He put this land in trust. It can't be sold or leased for a hundred years."

A hundred years! For a second, the gables on the Home in his dream shivered. The six small pillars on the front door shuddered, and the whole building almost came tumbling down in a heap at his feet.

After he had patiently endured, he obtained the promise. He had so patiently endured, and now when the whole world smelled like spring and the Down was blown like a cloud by the wind, where was the promise? He turned and looked the other way and saw nothing but the orphanage and the flat, treeless upland on either side of it, stretching away, nothing between it and the sky. Nothing between it and the sky!

Suddenly, he was off, furiously through the mud, spattering his shoes and his trousers.

"Mr. Müller? I say, where are you going? In all this mud?" The land agent started after him. "Sir, there's no need for you to take this out on our agency."

"Follow me," George called back in the wind. Rapidly, he paced off in front of the orphanage.

"In all this mud!" the agent muttered.

He would patiently endure. He would obtain the promise. "Ten . . . fifteen . . . twenty-five."

"My shoes, my new leather shoes! Insane!"

"One hundred ninety, two hundred," George explained, and turned to face the agent. "Two hundred!"

"I didn't count," the agent told him glumly.

"Two hundred on this side of the orphanage. And there must be two hundred on the other side. And two hundred yards is big enough frontage."

"Frontage? For what?"

"If I can't have that land down there, I'll build my Home right here."

"Next to your own building?" the agent asked, incredulously.

"So I won't have to trouble your agency for any land at all. I own all this already."

"But you can't," the agent sputtered.

"Why not? Two hundred yards is—"

"Is enough for just about half the structure you want to build."

"That's right. Just half," George said.

"What!"

"I'm not going to build one orphanage down there, sir, because I can't get the land. But you're not going to stop me from having my thousand orphans. I'll fool you. And everybody else that thinks God wants to limit George Müller. I'll build my orphanage in half. Half over there, and the other half over here; half on either side of what already stands."

The land agent opened his mouth and closed it again. But George looked back at him calmly, the front hair that always stood in a peak now disheveled in the wind, and he knew, beyond any doubt, that Henry had been wrong. With every fresh difficulty, God had a solution. And there didn't seem to be any limit.

Beyond any doubt at all, George Müller knew that God wanted him to build two new orphanages instead of one, and he didn't care in the least what people were going to say when they heard about it.

16

A Powerful Opponent

Actually, the final verdict rested with the architect hired to survey the property.

"Will it fit right in here beside the other?" George asked anxiously, while the architect set up strange, complicated gadgets on the orphanage lawn.

Momentarily, the architect looked like a reluctant orphan adding four and five. He squinted, and he cocked his headfirst to the left, then to the right. He ran a tongue tentatively over his upper lip and finally he nodded. "Like a fat man in a carriage. Just slide in and no room to spare. But it will fit all right. You can count on building the new place right there beside the old."

To patiently endure, and obtain the promise! "Thank You, God, for giving me this small bit of insight," was the silent note of praise. And then to the architect, "You draw up plans and we'll break ground by August."

By fall, the foundation was laid. Bricklayers, carpenters, and laborers came out from Bristol every day on the morning train and laid their bricks and fitted their beams twelve hours a day. The hammering and the banging and the shouting made his study noisier than the Bristol docks at high tide, but when he closed his window against it all, George felt no annoyance, only a kind of glee at what God was doing right in front of his eyes.

All fall, his excitement and joy got bigger and bigger. "December already, Mary. Five months' work done."

She set the bowl of thick beef stew at his place. "The post brought a letter this morning. But eat that stew before it gets cold. Your mail can wait."

He reached for the letter, blowing on the stew as he read it. "Mary, remember that contract for window glass?" The contract had been too high, and he had waited to sign it. "Looks like I waited too long."

Mary, her back to the stove, made a clucking sound that meant, "Now that's too bad."

"Too long for the contract," he said, exultantly. "Mary, this letter gives me all the glass I need for every window in the Home. Three hundred windows, Mary, unsolicited and free!"

So he had been in danger of going beyond his limit? As he went through his routine chores that fall—parish calls on Gideon Chapel folks, preaching and the steady supervision of orphanage affairs—he wanted to put his hands on the shoulders of everyone he met and say, "God knows no limits. And George Müller is only His channel. Listen to this and this and this!"

In just this kind of singing mood, he wrote in his journal on February 19, 1856: "Now at last, the Lord has been pleased to give me today 3,000 pounds. It is left to my disposal for the work of the Lord. I took 1,700 for the Building Fund."

And on March 18: "Received 4,000 pounds which were left at my disposal as the work of the Lord might require. For the Building Fund, I took 3,000 pounds."

And a year after that: "January 20, 1857, received 500 pounds, the disposal of which was left to me." By May 1857, Ashley Down had a new silhouette against the sky. A second chunky building squared off beside the first. It was almost ready for three hundred little girls from the rowdy slums of Bristol.

And as spring became summer, it seemed as if God still had not set His limits for George Müller and the children of Bristol.

"Mary, the gas burners are installed. And they work. I just tested them." George was talking before he closed the kitchen door behind him. "It's almost finished. But don't stop praying." He was half-joking with her. "We still need more money."

"A thousand pounds less than you needed at morning prayer," Mary called out from across the kitchen, her head in the great bake oven.

"How's that?"

"On the table. It came today."

He picked up an envelope. "This?"

"It's a thousand pounds." Mary turned her flushed face from the oven to George. "A thousand pounds. The gas burners are paid for now, anyway."

On November 12, 1857, the first orphan—a little girl with hair so matted that George had thought she was a bundle of West Indian hemp when he first saw her sleeping on the wharf— dropped her lumpy package of shredded underwear and a single doll on the floor of the second Home, looking scared to be so close to so much cleanness. It was all done, seven years after George had begun to pray.

It had cost 35,000 pounds from the first brick to the last gas burner.

And 35,335 pounds had been donated.

That meant—George chuckled to himself when he added it up and wondered if he dared point out some mathematical facts to Henry Craik—that God had gone 335 pounds beyond the limit George had set for himself! And no one had been asked for a shilling.

But George did not fritter away time clucking over what he knew was small change. He had bigger things on his mind. While the four hundred new girls were assigned beds in the second house, George's mind was racing ahead to the third—like a kite flown on the Down by the boys, leaping and prancing on and up and threatening to rip away from its owner!

It mounted higher and higher, beyond the plan for a Home housing three hundred, as he had first dreamed. And when

George sat down to talk to the architects, the wind was blowing wildly indeed!

At the long mahogany table in the Visitor's Room, the architects scribbled on paper, heads bent even after George had finished talking. "Well, answer my question," he repeated.

The chief architect turned to look at George, his eyes stopping midway at the man on his right to signal, *This man is a fanatic. I told you not to get mixed up with him. He's a raving religious fanatic.* To George, he spoke very patiently, as if he were explaining a blueprint to a 10-year-old. "But, Mr. Müller, our original agreement with you was to draw up plans for a third building to house three hundred."

"Answer my question. Would it cost more to house four hundred fifty?"

"But sir, originally—"

"Would it cost more?" he persisted.

The architect made angry little strokes on his paper. "No, sir. It wouldn't cost a great deal more. It's just that we—all of us—we had drawn up plans and—"

"All right. That's what I want to know. We'll build house number three the biggest yet. Three hundred orphans, that's not enough. We'll stretch this out for four hundred fifty." Let the architects grumble as they may. George Müller and God were going to pay the bills and they would buy exactly what they wanted to!

Shortly after, there was a gift of 7,000 pounds, and a month later, another of 1,700. More glass was donated for the 390 windows in the new Home. And in July 1859, the bricklayers, the carpenters, and the laborers swarmed up to the Down from Bristol once more.

Two years later the building was almost done, and when George added up his receipts, he discovered that 46,000 pounds had been given to the Building Fund. That was 11,000 more than he had prayed for! "Thank You, God, for not setting Your limit yet" was his joyful thought.

And in March 1862, it was finished. Now three buildings squatted substantially on Ashley Down. They had a well-scrubbed-orphan look about them, yet they weren't forlorn. Square and unornamented, their three stories were as practical as mutton. But here and there, a gable added an unobtrusive frill. To George, they looked as solid as the gospel. To him, they were beautiful.

More than a thousand parentless, homeless boys and girls, from six weeks to seventeen years old, now depended on George Müller for three meals a day, clothes to wear, and the only education they would ever get.

The staff increased too. By the time the third Home opened, George had acquired an assistant, a serious-minded young man named Jim Wright. George took to confiding in him almost as naturally as if he were talking to himself. When they met around the Homes, George had a way of falling in step with him and starting the conversation in the middle of whatever he had been thinking about.

One day in 1865, he met Jim coming out of the laundry room, and together they walked down the shadowy, cool basement corridor. "Five thousand pounds is the biggest single gift God has given me yet, Jim," George said.

Jim picked up his train of thought quickly. "And it's half of what you need to get started. It really begins to look as if God wants you to go ahead with it." He broke off, and behind his thick glasses, blinked his eyes.

"There was a doubt in your mind?" George asked quickly.

Jim hesitated. "Well, it is a pretty big undertaking, sir. Building two more orphanages, well—"

"So you too, Jim. All the time you've been wondering will the money come in for this, too? How long can he keep this up?"

"Well, sir, doubling the number of children here—being responsible for two thousand people—it makes a chap thoughtful."

"I don't build for the sake of building," George said quietly.

"I know, sir. And you'll do it yet, sir." Jim blinked rapidly. "Keep right on until you've got your five houses up here and room for two thousand orphans. You have your 5,000 pounds. More will come in." He spoke intensely, sincerely, but George knew that his faith came with an effort. "Slowly, maybe, but it will come. It might take years. Don't get discouraged, Mr. Müller."

"Thank you, Jim." They had come to the first floor, and George turned toward his study. "I'll remember those words tomorrow."

Jim blinked. "Tomorrow?"

"I have an appointment with an agent about buying some more land. You see, Jim, there's one difference between your trust and mine. Mine won't wait around for years. I have 5,000 now, and I expect the rest to come along any day. So I'm ready to talk about buying the land now. I want to get two more orphanages up as fast as I can."

The land he wanted lay directly across the road from the third Home. It stretched out for about eighteen acres, and it was flat and clear, except for a small house at one end. If he wanted to build, it was the logical spot. There was no other space left on the Down.

But the angular land agent had other ideas, and he stated them, facing George across his desk. Fingering his pale blue scarf nervously, he said, "I do wish you wouldn't blame our agency, Mr. Müller. It's simply not our fault that the property you want is unavailable."

"Then who wants it? It isn't very valuable. Such mud in the spring. With a little bit of coaxing, it would be under water."

"That's just it," the agent said, cryptically.

George swung around. "What do you mean?"

"Let me explain. First, to get this property you would have to contend with three people. The tenant."

"Tenant? There's nobody on that land!"

The agent's thin finger plucked at his neck scarf, then patted it back in place again. "But nevertheless there is a tenant. He has the land leased until 1867. Two more years."

George shrugged. "That all? That's not quite like a hundred. Give me his name. I'll talk to him. Show him I must have the land, or there can't be a new orphanage."

"Even if you convinced him, you'll have trouble with the owner." All this worry about men seemed irrelevant. He had seen so many miracles, and yet this anemic land agent talked about a tenant and an owner with so much despair. "The owner has set his purchase price at 7,000 pounds," he heard the agent say.

Seven thousand was 2,000 more than he had figured. The owner couldn't be shrugged away, then. But even so, there had been so many miracles already.

"Who is the third?" George asked.

"Somebody with whom you can't argue, Mr. Müller. Some-one—" The land agent smiled nervously, and then jerked his lips back to somberness again. "Someone considered by many as powerful as the Almighty Himself."

"Who's that?"

"It's the House of Parliament, sir! The Bristol Waterworks has its eyes on that land too. Wants to turn it into a city reservoir."

"Parliament? The Waterworks?" George repeated numbly. "I don't understand."

"The Waterworks wants an act passed to set aside that plot of land for city use. Permanently! Parliament is already working on it. No, Mr. Müller, I'm sorry to disappoint you, but you see it's impossible for you to build any more orphanages on Ashley Down."

If God were trying to show him his spiritual limit, He was surely doing it with a flourish that would convince any true Britisher. George thought in amusement, "But I'm not a Britisher. I'm a foreigner."

17

The Bristol Waterworks

The Bristol Waterworks' offices smelled faintly like a cellar that people have kept closed for a long time for their own reasons. George looked for green mold on the black suits of the Waterworks officials, seated rigidly behind identical desks. There were Mr. Hawser, Mr. Johnson, and Mr. Wilkins.

Mr. Hawser was obviously the man to deal with.

He took the lead in the conversation, lacing one long-fingered hand into the other and cracking his knuckles. "Mr. Müller, it was very wise of you not to go up to London before approaching our offices here." His words were soft, nasal at the same time, and pronounced in a kind of singsong that made a long sentence twice as long.

George sat down on an uncomfortable chair. Mr. Hawser went on. "Now then, you wish to purchase a lot on Ashley Down on which to build a Home for the care and shelter of dependent children?"

"It's the only suitable land left up there," George began.

"Mr. Wilkins, include that in your record." There was some furious scribbling at the third desk on the left.

"To continue, the Bristol Waterworks, an agent of the government of the city of Bristol and established for these seventy-five years"—George edged forward on the chair, ready to pounce into the flow of words—"has had as its purpose the good of all citizens of the city. Not just a small specialized and selective group." Snapping knuckles capitalized his meaning. "Do you see?"

"Yes, but I—" With despair, George realized that Hawser's mouth was moving again.

"I want to make it very clear to you that our two organizations—yours and mine—are so very diverse. Yours, philanthropy. Ours, a function of the government. Therefore, it would be unthinkable that we should stoop to dicker."

A brief prayer went up at the Waterworks office. "God, stop his mouth long enough for me to tell him that the city desperately needs two more orphanages."

Hawser was still talking. "Now there seems to have been a misunderstanding on your part, Mr. Müller. You seem to feel that you have some right to question our interest in the aforementioned parcel of land on Ashley Down."

George jumped at this chance. "I'm not questioning. But I

wanted a chance to explain how badly we need another Home. You see—"

But Hawser intoned, "Whereas in reality, Mr. Müller, there is nothing to be gained by your so doing. My dear fellow, let me make it very clear and simple to you. You have been misinformed."

"What?" George broke in. "About Parliament? You aren't—?"

The knuckles cracked again. "Of course we are. But only for the smallest fraction of the property you wish to purchase."

"But—but—"

"Someone gave you the wrong information, dear chap. We want only a tiny portion of the land you want to buy. Not enough to hinder your building. The rest of our land is down the hill."

On his right, Mr. Johnson nodded. On his left, Mr. Wilkins nodded, and wrote something on the records.

"Gentlemen," and George stood up to leave, "may God bless your reservoir as He has blessed my orphanages. Good day!"

He went next to see the tenant, and the address scribbled on a piece of paper was the slums beyond the Cathedral. As he passed St. Mary Redcliffe, he hardly glanced up at the arches and porches. He had seen them often, and their intricate fretwork only made him nervous. Yet people had called the Bristol Cathedral beautiful since the thirteenth century and came for miles to see it. George preferred the square solidity of his Homes or the Gideon Chapel. It seemed to him that real beauty should not call a man's thoughts away from God.

Beyond the Cathedral, what he saw in the slums pleased him much less. A ragged girl stopped him for a shilling. A boy with a crooked arm played with a pig in the gutter. The sight of it all sent him hurrying across lanes, up alleys, looking for the man who had leased the Ashley Down acres.

To George's surprise, he found a hunched old man. Perhaps because he had been bent so many years like a question mark, his sentences all ended querulously on a high note. It gave an irritable sound to what he said.

"Blimey, Reverend, I don't see why you even ask me. It's my land by tenant rights, and I don't aim to give it up."

"But you don't even have a cottage up there, sir."

"Don't need no cottage to make it mine. I paid two years' rent for it, and that makes it mine."

"If you even had a little garden on the land—"

The old man peered up at George, and he raised his fist as if he wanted to shake it, then dropped it again. "Who's to say I won't? I been laid up with the rheumatism all winter, but come next year, I just might have a garden."

Just might have a garden! While children played with pigs in the gutter? George tried to break through the man's irritability. He told him about the orphanages he had built already, the new ones he planned for a thousand children, children who might be living right there on Blackheart Street. For twenty minutes, George talked.

The old man said nothing. Finally he sniffed. "Not my children, they ain't." He was unmoved. "Why should I have to pay for them?"

Apparently, the old man's heart was as shriveled as his chest. George had already turned away when he heard the last words. Pay for them?

"Sir, every shilling you paid for rent on that land, I'll give it back to you. Do you understand that?"

The old man said doggedly, "But I paid all of the next two years."

"And I'll pay you back."

"Well, why didn't you say so?" Now the old man was grinning.

"Then we've made a bargain?"

"Blimey, 'course it's a bargain. I'm not one for starving little children, Reverend. But it didn't seem quite cricket—the missus and me losing those two years of rent."

George left the old man grinning, his crooked back bobbing up and down, and picked his way down Blackheart Street around three cats snarling over a piece of meat on the pavement.

The owner of the eighteen acres was next. "I won't come down. Not one shilling. Seven thousand is my price."

"The land isn't worth a shilling more than five thousand," George said. And then to himself, "God, make me shrewd and keep me honest!"

"Not worth it? Then why are you so anxious, my friend?"

"Because it suits my purpose. Five thousand."

"Seven thousand." The owner smiled like the Blackheart Street cat who won the meat.

"If you don't take my offer, you'll go looking for a buyer. In the spring, it's nothing but mud up there. Five thousand."

"Six thousand five hundred."

"Five thousand two hundred. No higher." Again to himself, "This is Your money, God. Tell me how to spend it."

"You're a robber," the owner told him candidly. "Six thousand two hundred."

"Five thousand two hundred."

"Six thousand." The price slid down. "That's final!"

"Five thousand five hundred."

"Five thousand nine." The owner was coming down.

"God, help me to know how long he'll bargain!" was his anguished thought. "Five thousand five," George repeated.

"Five thousand seven," said the owner, scowling.

George pounced. "Five thousand seven. Not a pound more."

"I'm giving you a bargain." The owner did not smile.

"Not you," George told him. "It's God who gives the bargain. Come, let's sign the papers."

Before the first shovel dug into Ashley Down soil, there were a few disappointments. George had planned to build his fourth house first, his fifth later, as the money was given. With enough to finance the fourth one, he brought the contractor up from Bristol to talk about building.

With a lack of patience, the contractor explained to him what he said, crossly, George should have known. To do the job in two installments would almost double the cost. And the Building Fund did not then have the price of building both Homes at once.

"Then there's only one thing to do," George decided, reluctantly. "You'll have to go home now and come back when I do have the money to build two houses at once."

"It's a fine time to tell me that. When do you figure you'll be calling me?"

"Who knows?" George answered. "I'll ask God, and when He tells me, by sending me the money I need, I'll come to your house and tell you."

The contractor looked at him as if he were a mad man and started the long descent back to Bristol.

It was disappointing the way the money came in. A shilling from a mill worker, a sovereign from one of the orphans, 5 pounds from a schoolteacher.

A whole year dragged by that way. "To glorify You, God," George prayed. The greatest monument of all! Room for a thousand more children!

"A Father to the fatherless."

"Open thy mouth wide, and I will fill it."

"After he had patiently endured, he obtained the promise." He clung to these verses.

He couldn't stop believing now. Nor would he turn to anybody in Bristol for help. "To prove You are faithful, Lord! Four thousand years ago, and today as well!" again his plea. And the money came in, slowly, but gradually. On May 7, 1866, shovels bit into the chalky Down soil. The orphanage was underway.

Standing as close to the digging as he could, George exulted in this new miracle. Now there would be five buildings to throw a shadow across the Down, a shadow so big it would almost seem like the shadow of the Almighty Himself, walking on the hills up from Bristol. And all Ashley Down would become a children's village, a town of children who had been lifted up away from the dirt and disease and the Devil himself down there in the slums.

As he stood there with Jim Wright beside him, he was praying a prayer of intense thanksgiving. Then Jim interrupted, "There's your wife coming up the hill, sir."

But he had told Mary to stay home. She had been coughing all week. Yet there she was, bustling up the hill toward them.

"There's Lydia too." Jim pointed down the hill. But Lydia had stopped to watch the digging from there. "Lydia," George said with a sigh. "Sometimes I look at her from far off as now, and I ask myself what about the Lydia who wanted a wide-open place with breezes? Is she really happy now that she's grown up? If she could only find a husband—" He broke off. "Jim, this worry interrupts my happiness."

"Maybe someday she will." But Jim wasn't listening.

Now Mary was almost up the hill, coughing, turning her head away, pretending to be intent on the digging so George wouldn't see the violence of her cough.

"Mary," he called out as she came closer, "I told you to stay home and keep warm."

She was almost at the brink of the hill where the Down leveled off to a plateau. "Miss this? Not if they had to carry me up!" She laughed, and then coughed again.

"You better take care of that cold, Mrs. Müller," Jim said. "My wife didn't. She's running a fever."

"You see, Mary." George took his eyes from the shovels and looked at her intently. As she sewed dresses and carried blankets from one house to the others, he couldn't stop her any more than he knew how to discipline a roomful of pillow-fighting eight-year-olds.

"Now don't start scolding, George. Not today. Don't tell me I work too hard—" But her cough kept her from protesting.

"There. Take care of yourself—at least for me, Mary."

"Now don't be so sentimental," she said briskly. "I'll live to see your orphanage finished and the curtains hung! After that, well, we'll worry about that when it comes." She coughed again harder, but George was watching the workmen this time. He didn't see her shoulders shaking, and the clanging of the shovels and the shouts of the men drowned out the sound of her cough.

It took four years to build the fourth and fifth Homes. But on January 6, 1870, they were both finished. Now 2,050 parentless children would have a Christian home and education.

The wind buffeted George and Mary about as they stood atop the Down that January day, but they weren't ready to go inside the Home yet. Out on the Down, with its wide-open feeling, its smell of the sea, its spirit of yearning over the dirty city below, they could marvel. And it was a day for marveling.

For George knew that on that day his monument to a God who still broods over life on earth was finished. He had accomplished the first and primary goal of his life. He had built five orphanages, he was providing for two thousand orphans, and he was doing it all by prayer and faith. In all the years he had never asked anyone for a shilling!

It was done at last. The buildings would stand half a century or more after he died, and everyone who knew about them would also learn that every brick had been prayed there.

They had called him independent, a rebel, even a fanatic. Maybe some who heard the story in another time, in another land, would call him simple and have their doubts. But to many more, it would be a sign. As he stood on the Down that day, he was certain of that.

"They will *know*, Mary!"

She turned and looked at him affectionately. "Know what, George?"

"That God is faithful still and hears prayer still."

"Why, of course—" she started to say, but a cough interrupted the sentence.

He took her arm. "You belong inside," he said. "With our orphans." And together they walked into the newest building on Ashley Down.

18

Monument to a Faithful God

A month later, Mary Müller was dead. George was left alone with his daughter, Lydia, and the orphans. But even though he was sixty-five, life was not over for him. A year and a half later, Jim Wright, whose wife had also died, confided to George that he and Lydia had fallen in love. A few weeks after that, George surprised his daughter and future son-in-law by announcing that he too was going to remarry—Susannah Grace Sanger, whom he had known at the Gideon Chapel for twenty-five years.

Susannah Müller was in her early forties when George married her, and she convinced him that he had health enough to realize his earliest dreams of taking the gospel to the mission field. When he was seventy-one, he and Susannah started out on a series of missionary trips to Europe, Asia, and America. He traveled 200,000 miles, preached in forty-two countries, and kept up this pace until he was 88!

He died at Ashley Down when he was 93. The day before he died, he was still handling orphanage correspondence and protesting that he felt fine.

After George's death, Jim Wright and Lydia took charge of the orphanage. They too are dead now, but the children's work in Bristol still goes on.

Always, George prayed that after his death the Homes would not be tied to outworn traditions. He would be happy to know that now, the brick dormitories having been sold, all the children are housed in many small cottages, to give them the atmosphere of a Christian home.

But the work, with its headquarters in Bristol, still conducts no financial campaigns, and still trusts God for its support. Today, as in George Müller's time well over a hundred years ago, it is a monument to a very faithful God.

Epilogue

George Müller cared for 10,000 orphans during his lifetime. After his death, his ministry continued at the complex of buildings on Ashley Hill, where another 7,000 orphans received care until the facility closed. If you travel to Bristol, England, today, you can still see the buildings and visit the George Müller Museum.

Though he never made appeals for money, he raised about $2.5 million to support his ministry to vulnerable children. In today's dollars, that amount is worth about $180 million. The George Müller Charitable Trust continues his vision today, helping young people and families through local churches. Like its founder, the trust never asks for money, trusting God to provide for needs.

Most importantly, George Müller's ideas continue to inspire the generations after his death. "God is faithful still and hears prayers still."

More Inspiring, True Stories

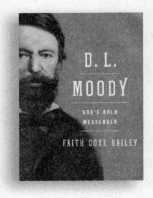

A fascinating biography of an ordinary man who lived for God and became the greatest evangelist of the nineteenth century.

D. L. Moody dared to take up a challenge and see what God could do with a life totally committed to Him. Here is the story of the greatest American evangelist of the 1800's and the founder of the Moody Bible Institute.

Also available as an eBook

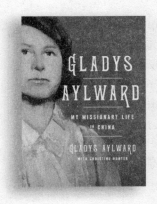

A solitary woman.
A foreign country.
An unknown language.
An impossible dream? No.

A true story of a determined missionary, *Gladys Aylward: My Missionary Life in China* will challenge you to have bold and expectant faith.

Also available as an eBook and audiobook

MOODY
Publishers®

From the Word to Life®